CHANGE

~~~ is ~~~

GREAT

CHANGE

~~ is ~~

GREAT

BE
FIRST

RICHARD M. BATENBURG, JR.

Advantage®

Published by Advantage, Charleston, South Carolina.
Member of Advantage Media Group.

ADVANTAGE is a registered trademark and the Advantage colophon is a trademark of Advantage Media Group, Inc.

Printed in the United States of America.

ISBN: 978-1-59932-567-5
LCCN: 2015951546

This publication is designed to provide accurate and authoritative information in regard to the subject matter covered. It is sold with the understanding that the publisher is not engaged in rendering legal, accounting, or other professional services. If legal advice or other expert assistance is required, the services of a competent professional person should be sought.

Advantage Media Group is proud to be a part of the Tree Neutral® program. Tree Neutral offsets the number of trees consumed in the production and printing of this book by taking proactive steps such as planting trees in direct proportion to the number of trees used to print books. To learn more about Tree Neutral, please visit **www.treeneutral.com**. To learn more about Advantage's commitment to being a responsible steward of the environment, please visit **www.advantagefamily.com/green**

Advantage Media Group is a publisher of business, self-improvement, and professional development books and online learning. We help entrepreneurs, business leaders, and professionals share their Stories, Passion, and Knowledge to help others Learn & Grow. Do you have a manuscript or book idea that you would like us to consider for publishing? Please visit **advantagefamily.com** or call **1.866.775.1696**.

To my bride, Judy, who made this all possible.

ABOUT THE AUTHOR

Richard M. Batenburg Jr. is an operations-oriented executive with proven success in managing all aspects of business, from strategic through tactical planning and execution. He has more than thirty years of experience in various industries, including television, film, and live show production as CEO/COO, owner, and operator. His communication skills have been developed over years of directing the marketing, sales, promotion, publicity, and public relations for both public and private companies.

Richard has honed his leadership capabilities through streamlining technology infrastructure, business processes, and practices and establishing strategies to maximize the company's profitability while reducing overall costs.

His business background includes successfully planning and managing the integration and assimilation of marketing, sales, and operations in many organizations as part of merger activity of large, medium, and small public and private companies.

Richard's particular focus is on the "end to end" processes used by the frontline employees in enterprise to deliver products and services to customers. He is the principal owner and cofounder of BATMANN Consulting, Inc. and Cliintel, LLC, both organically grown from his basement over the past 15 years, providing solution services to large enterprise in the pursuit of changing the way business is measured by management and delivered by the frontline employee.

Richard lives in Denver, Colorado, with his wife and three children. He is an avid ice hockey player, a Colorado Avalanche season ticket holder, and a die-hard Detroit Red Wings fan.

ACKNOWLEDGMENTS

I would like to acknowledge the staggering number of people with whom I have worked over the course of my career at The Armadillo Club, Waddell and Reed, The Garment District, Comedy Works, Comedy Core, First Films, First Entertainment, Video Communications and Radio, VideOne Marketing, BATMANN Productions, BPI, TCI, REN, AT&T Broadband, Comcast, Sun Microsystems, BATMANN Consulting, BATMANN Analytics, and Cliintel—literally thousands of interesting, creative, energetic people—all representing the true fabric of my career.

First and foremost, I thank my wife, customer, financier, collaborator, and best friend, Judy, as well as my kids Rick, Leigh, and Faith for all the support and forgiveness for the events I missed due to the time I spent building companies. Thanks to my parents, Dick and Marita Batenburg, for teaching me about work ethic and its importance.

Thanks to my long-time business partner and friend Mark Radtke (a.k.a. Mr. 100 percent), who for 15 years has never failed to support and believe. Mark is the foundation and practitioner of our business culture because he is the best people person with whom I have ever had the privilege to work.

Continuing thanks to all the colleagues, past and present, who choose to spend time working with me and our clients, which leads me to some extra special people:

Scott Shippy (a.k.a. The Boss). As a serial entrepreneur, I found it hard to work for "the man"—this is one man I have and would again work for—he is also one of the big reasons this book was written. Without his suggestion, it would not have been seriously pursued.

Steve Stainbrook—the best customer, colleague, and friend anyone could hope for—courageous and demanding, firm and fair ... possibly the calmest, most practical executive I have ever done business with.

Kris Pogue—former bookkeeper and trusted financial advisor, currently fighting and beating the big C—brave to the point of fearless, mentally tough, tender-hearted, and a straight-shooting accountant.

Inspiring former teammates: Lauri Smith, Crystal Allen, Matt Eidemiller, Bill Shaw, Vince DiBiase, Steve Hobbs, Paul Ousterhout, Richie Schoenmaker, Davyd Smith, Mike Kellim, Anne Mckissick, Marie LeMoine, Lisa Woitalewicz, Gillian Willis, Matt Harvey, Kelly Oberbillig, Susie Love, Roxanne Guidichessi, Wende Curtis, Suzanne Godovic, Russ Schlager, and Billy Anderson.

I must acknowledge the members and chair of Vistage group CE 3513, whose wisdom, guidance, and counsel have been invaluable since I had the good fortune to join the CE 3513 in 2009—Christiaan Vandenberg, Peter Horewitch, John Gibson, Martin Faith, Kirk Darfler, Jeff Sippel, Randy Schrader, Dave Cole, Stephanie Klein, Mariano Delle Donne, Beatriz Bonnet, Richard Bryan, Steve Williams, David Gaudet, and Thomas Mair.

To my assistant, Abigail Klass—the personification of a person at peace, wise beyond her years, and the only reason I get anything actually finished on time. To all the employees at Cliintel, who demonstrate every day the "WHY" it's important to embrace change and... BE FIRST!

Thanks to you all.

Bat

PREFACE

Why Write a Book?

I finally committed to writing a book in an attempt to formalize and explain what has become our (Cliintel, LLC) "solution" offering. The ideas contained herein were not born from scientific research but through actual practice over the past 30 years in companies public and private, small to enormous, retail (B2C) and commercial (B2B).

The ideas, while simple—perhaps commonsensical—are challenging to implement because they require human beings to change. I have a background in the stand-up comedy business and an undergraduate degree in psychology, so here is the second of my three favorite jokes; while normally told in sequence, the first and third are too blue for publication!

How many psychologists does it take to change a light bulb?

Just one, but the light bulb must want to change!

Working smart is certainly a component of the ideas in this book, as is working hard and with purpose. The real work of management is to motivate people to do things. In this age, it's simply not enough to pay for performance or provide nifty offices and benefits. This book is about how servant leadership, culture, teamwork, measurement, and execution with sensitivity to the human condition is the way for any company to create a culture that embraces change, thus creating an environment that is rewarding, empowering, and engaging for all the humans within.

TABLE OF CONTENTS

Chapter 8

Chapter 9

Chapter 10

In Closing

INTRODUCTION

If you read the books about real visionaries—people such as John D. Rockefeller Sr. or Steve Jobs—you discover that one of the things those guys had in common was not only having big egos but also a plan to get there. Everyone talks about the importance of embracing a BHAG (Big Hairy Audacious Goal) or big visions, and conceptually, that's great advice. What is missing is the connectivity between "Where I am today" and "Where I want to be"—let's say, going to the moon. So how do you get there? The first questions emerge as, "Who can help me travel the next 20 feet, and who's going to support me on the next mile and a half?" If it's 250,000 miles away, you can get there, but you're going to need help. You're going to need to stay the course, and, most importantly, you must stick to your vision.

It's the same thing with change in your corporate culture. First, you start with awareness that you want and need to change. Then you need to sit down and do the tactical planning. Sometimes you find you took a wrong turn. Can you pick yourself up and readjust your course?

Where executives in most companies go astray is that they can't come back to center and refocus, or they don't have the commitment to change that is necessary to overcome the hurdles. An executive must come to the realization that the company cannot reach the summit of a mountain when they can't possibly scale it. They must, instead, find the patience to walk around it.

How committed are you? How "in" is "all in"? Everybody wants a piece of a successful company, and that's why many people join big companies; I like to call it the "warm blanket of enterprise." Up until a decade or two ago, most people worked for the same enterprise for years, even decades, with that warm blanket around them, to the point where they no longer realized that the blanket was there, and they took it for granted. In recent history, people began changing employers with more regularity ... and the frequency of change is increasing. Ever since downsizing or 'rightsizing' and 'outsourcing' became culturally accepted, the norm of staying with one company long enough to get a gold watch has all but disappeared. When people leave an employer for a startup or to start their own business (another popular pursuit), they are thinking that they will be just as effective without the support systems and infrastructure—without the warm blanket of enterprise. Very often they fail because they don't respect and understand the virtues of the company ecosystem, and they simply don't value anything other than their piece of it.

When they're immersed in the ecosystem of enterprise, people may see that something needs to be fixed, but they can't see a way to get that change in motion; they can't see a clear pathway across the mountain. So they sit down, defeated.

Change or die is the way of the of business world we now live and work in. Time to get up—*be first!*

CHAPTER 1

WHY BE FIRST?

A case for courage in the face of the status quo.

Change is the law of life. And those who look only to
the past or present are certain to miss the future.
—John F. Kennedy

E verybody wants to talk about change, especially leaders; the higher they are on the food chain, the more they like to talk about change. That's a symptom of the fact that they are not the ones who have to change. When you're up at C-level, there is a lot of talk about "how we need to change," but the "we" is everyone else. The motto is, "Change is great—you go first." C-level executives are always interested in adopting whatever change methodology my company (Cliintel) is pitching, until it comes down to actually changing themselves—and that's when the wheels come off.

The impact of disruption starts to enter the client's mind, and they say, "Well, we can't do it right now," or "Maybe next year, maybe next quarter." In the fourth quarter, they say, "We haven't got our budgets yet," or my personal favorite, "We have our budgets now, and this change project didn't make it in."

Coupled with this particular observation is the fact that when our consulting team talks to an individual, no matter what their rank in the hierarchical command structure, they are initially very interested in the concept of change-related improvement. When we get another person at the table from the organization, the interest starts to get watered down, and by the time we have a third person at the table, magically, all of the problems have disappeared and no real change is necessary.

That's symptomatic of two things: one is that humans generally don't like change, but the bigger one has to do with peer pressure and lack of trust within the organization from department to department, or within the hierarchical command structure, because people don't want to admit that they need help. They'll discuss the issues, but as far as root cause, it will be hung on a department or person who is not in the room. That's why internal change must begin by building trust between the organizational structures, from silo to silo and within the hierarchical command structure, before anyone can implement any kind of change effort. In big organizations, the whole concept of having courage to make decisions is related to the political environment where you are operating, which is why there are so many books about driving politics out of organizations; it's the killer of change.

The fact of the matter is that the consumer has already changed, and if you're not on board to meet their evolving needs and demands, then you'll be passed by when a more nimble, people-centric company comes nipping at your heels.

THE NEW WORLD ORDER AND HOW WE GOT HERE

When we talk about the creation of the multinational conglomerate or the large enterprise environment, we have Henry Ford and other large industrialists to thank and blame. Mobility—being able to move people, information, and goods—made the world flatter, and the Internet finished the job. Now we move information around with a keystroke; a 12-year-old can sell goods to someone in China from his living room.

Obviously, that capability didn't exist in 1920; everything was corner stores—franchising was not a widely deployed business structure, and giant corporations were just starting. The advent of big corporations is really the maturation of distribution channels. That's where business started weighing the reduction of quality to allow the emergence of commoditized pricing. The Industrial Revolution was about increasing margins by getting scale: Manufacturing interchangeable parts at scale and then being able to distribute them enabled large corporations to be built. Those companies got bigger and bigger, as well as more and more removed from their customer, and the connection with the consumer was limited to advertising and marketing. With the mom-and-pop operations, customers knew that the buck stopped with the guy or gal behind the counter. I am not sure anybody knows where the buck stops with General Motors. That's the dehumanizing part of the new standard of business; it's dispassionate, impersonal, and disconnected.

That's really what businesspeople have been trying to combat for the last 20 years, trying to use technology to rehumanize this relationship. But technology is not human, so it's a poor substitute. All it does is allow more scale and more excuses, and the customer is still left to deal with these big nameless, faceless corporations. The consumer didn't make companies that way; they made themselves that way. Companies chose to be nameless and faceless when consumers told them that what they really wanted was lower prices. Companies figured out how to give lower prices to the consumer, albeit at the expense of quality and service. Now, we as consumers are rebelling against the drive for price at the expense of quality; we want to have our cake and eat it too. But we don't always like the cake once we have it. Right now we're in the throes of that paradigm shift in which companies need to lead their customers in a partnership capacity and build the trust bridge between themselves and their customers.

In the 1980s, companies reached critical mass; we saw the rise of many multinational, multistate companies that had literally hundreds of thousands of employees, all dehumanized in their contact with the customers. What follows from that is dehumanizing the contact within the organization because they are so big. Once I, as a CEO or a C-level or VP-level executive, treat everybody like a number, it's easy for me to reduce vital messaging down to memos and remove the messy part of communication that makes it effective—which is the collaboration, the buy-in agreement.

Remember when you were a kid and your parents ended arguments with, "Because I said so"? It felt unreasonable then, but if you have kids, you've probably used that same phrase. The fact remains, though, that people need to understand the "why." Customers need to know the "why" so they can understand their options. Employees need to know the "why" so that they can find meaning in their jobs.

That's become even truer with the millennial generation; some would suggest that they are lazy, but I think a more accurate interpretation is that they don't want to do stuff until they understand the "why" of it. (see Fig. 1)

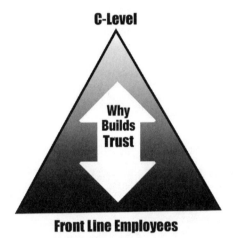

C-Level

Why Builds Trust

Front Line Employees

"Trust is a two-way street."

Figure 1

The baby boomers, born (roughly) between 1940 and 1964 are, for the most part, the bulk of the "in command" portion of the current workforce. Boomers believe in more, more, more: markets will always be increasing because, with two or three exceptions, that's how it's always been. Boomers haven't dealt much with long-lasting, dramatic change. When there was change in their formative years, 15-20 years of age, it began and ended abruptly in a violent correction (such as the stock market, for example), and boomers didn't handle such changes very well. Essentially, Boomers don't like change because they are currently "in charge" and have the most invested in the current systems—which they designed!

Clearly, change is going to happen. So do you plan for it and ride the wave, or do you stand against the wind until you get blown over? You can take option two, but there's no guarantee you'll be able to get back up.

CHAPTER 2

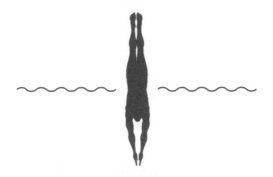

BRUTE FORCE MANAGEMENT

Why issuing a memo (via email) with a "directive"
simply doesn't work anymore.

*Customer service, they say, is dead. Actually, it isn't.
It's just hiding behind a call center in Manila.*
—Timothy Noah

THE HATED FIVE

There are five industries almost universally hated by their customers. Banks, airlines, utilities, and phone and cable companies—what do they have in common? To begin with, they were all born as either monopolies or highly regulated entities, and they are all necessities of modern life. They did not have to participate in the free market economy as described by the economist Adam Smith's "invisible hand" theory of markets in his 1776 book, *An*

Inquiry into the Nature and Causes of the Wealth of Nations. Because of regulation, they enjoyed protections that prohibited the normal free market pressures and controls from being applied to their industries. Without that free market pressure, there are distortions in the business process that would ordinarily evolve had those pressures been present; simple things, like actually caring about the customer.

How is that indifference to the customer manifested? Let's start with how these businesses actually refer to customers. In the airline industry you're a "seat"; in the utility industries, they deliver power and water to "meters"; the phone company bills a "number," and in cable they bill a "house"; in banking, you are an account number—and yes, that's how they think of you. There were no humans involved in this equation when these businesses were started, because they didn't have to care about the customer. They didn't have to convince anyone that they needed electricity or water or that they couldn't fly themselves to Chicago by flapping their arms. Remember cable television in the 1970s and 1980s? We willingly waited months to get cable. Now that's changed, as new technologies such as satellite and IPTV have emerged to provide competition. In telephony, technology entered with a much better product, the wireless telephone, many people do not have a landline anymore.

The point is, change marches on, and eventually customers win the day, or at least they have a voice. The result is that companies change, adapt, and listen to their customers and give the people what they want—sometimes before they know they want it (think Apple)—or the company lags behind or crumbles. Changing that DNA is a long and involved process, since the companies in the "hated 5" grew to scale and weren't built to care about or even acknowledge the customer. The back office systems were built to support that environment: human systems, IT systems, business processes, and workflows. The only time the customer hears from one of the hated 5 is when they have to pay their bill, which is a negative experience. Never mind that the customer is angry because the company fails to deliver on its promises; the company/service provider has never had to worry about how the customer really feels because, at that specific moment in time, there was unfettered opportunity. Consequently, as competition arrives through technological advances or the lack of government protection or new disruptive technology, suddenly they have to work to keep their customers because somebody new is taking them.

The first step to change is acknowledging that you have a problem. Then the hurdle becomes the legacy systems: the processes, procedures, IT systems, etc. All the systems designed to deliver the product or service were built without regard for the customer. The companies have gotten so big and have so many customers that changing any of those institutionalized processes will be highly disruptive. Couple that with natural resistance to change by the humans within the system, and you have doubled the effort that you need to even introduce change, let alone actually implement it.

In my observation, executives resort first and foremost to brute force deployment, because that's the most efficient from a standpoint of introduction, but it doesn't get change adopted. Why? Well, because the humans in the system *are* human, and they push back against change. Brute force is an industrial revolutionary response to a problem because when it all began, labor was cheap and advances in technology were somewhat easy, so it was a big free for all. But we have reached capacity with speed and cost. We're in the era of abundance, where cheap labor is not available. So what do you do?

Clearly, quality, service, or both will suffer—or you have to raise prices. Now big companies—and smaller companies, too—are left playing catch-up, trying to figure out how to make what they do less disembodied and more customer-centric. Having first acknowledged that the company has a problem and that the problem has many facets, the company must also accept that it cannot work on all problems at once through a brute force deployment. The memo from on high, well intentioned as it may be, is impossible to execute at a tactical level.

WHAT'S IN IT FOR ME?

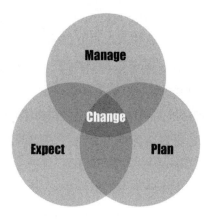

Figure 2

Here's a story I love that illustrates this point: There was a high-powered sales manager at a computer company that was terrifically successful and growing like crazy. This gentleman was unbeatable at building territory and increasing gross revenues. He was rewarded with all the baubles and trappings of that success. He was promoted rapidly through the organization, and at some point it was suggested that he go to Spain, open that market, and build the business. He went with vigor to Spain, and he decided after six months there that the problem was *siesta* and that *siesta* would be canceled forthwith. He was fired shortly after that. Siesta, after all, has been around about 2,000 years in Spain. It was probably a bit more change than one highly decorated general could pull off with a memo. But he did try, with all seriousness.

This is a prime example of the hubris of the brute force deployment. It's an indictment of the executive tendency to oversimplify the solution after finding a root cause. Just because you have found root cause doesn't mean you have found a cure or that the cure is as simple as "surgery" to remove a tool, process, or person. There are usually multiple components.

That's why a change effort that will work must contain a well-thought-out plan that is focused on adoption, not on eradicating root cause as its primary function. Eradicating root cause is the goal; it is not an operation implementation plan. The big idea here is that you want to create a *culture* of change, rather than a series of brute force deployments or a series of projects. It should be a cultural component of the company's existence that manages, expects, and plans for constant change. Figure 2 shows that successful change is the intersection of planning and expectation management.

Company leaders must make the effort if they don't want to join the dinosaurs in extinction, because whether or not they choose to move on, their customers are already considering a change.

CHAPTER 3

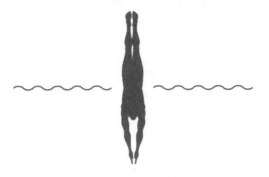

LIVING IN A CARFAX WORLD

Time to admit that the world is changing
and why you need to as well.

*Today, companies have to radically revolutionize themselves every few
years just to stay relevant. That's because technology and the Internet
have transformed the business landscape forever. The fast-paced
digital age has accelerated the need for companies to become agile.*
—Nolan Bushell

Business is constantly changing—but customer need/desire changes even faster, and corporate cultures are stuck playing catch-up. Even if you don't want to believe that there is a different way of doing things, you have to accept that your customers and competition are smarter than they used to be—and now candor, virtue, and values are being tested. As a business, you are more accountable to your customer today than ever before.

The Internet provides a world of data to everybody. As a result, customers have access to far more detailed information than internal sales organizations and the sales support organizations for the vendors selling the product—because, today, the customer has an army of millions sharing information/opinion outside the message conduit of the company. It's a CarFax world; everyone thinks they know the value and price of everything, or they believe they can find it instantly. Yes, sales organizations have access to the same information; however, because of the diversity of the products and services they represent, the sheer volume of information acts as a disadvantage, whereas an individual customer is prepared with a focused, researched, and evaluated need unique to them.

And it is not just about price or availability; it is about quality... and service. Consider the facility of preparing and reading reviews on products on the channel partner-type websites, with Amazon being the prime example. The increasing presence of online shopping certainly has a lot to do with convenience, in addition to price, but mostly because of the ability to weigh options based on others' feedback. It used to be that you told two friends and they told two friends, and that's how a company built an audience: via word of mouth. Now, it's done via the Internet, where everyone goes to look for product and service reviews before they buy—and the reviews are from strangers, not friends or even acquaintances: "Tom T. in Wendover says this is an awesome left-handed monkey wrench." Now, one review is unlikely to convince anyone, but if there are 75 reviews, your customers will read them and draw their own conclusions. With so much data available, everybody has become a data analyst.

What have companies done as a result of this? Some of them go and hire extremely cheap labor overseas to sit and write reviews of their products, reviews written by people who have never seen the product, let alone used it. There is a lot of disinformation out there and a lot of calories spent by some companies trying to cheat the system. What if you just spent that money on figuring out what your customers really want by getting close to them? The attempt to manipulate data can work in the short term, but it will ultimately fail to develop a long-term relationship. Customers are so well informed they will catch on and—with poetic justice—use the voice provided by the information superhighway to destroy the company and move on.

What does that mean in practice? Well, it probably means that the company is going to have to advertise and sell differently because the consumer can now pretty much call you on the carpet and globally trash your reputation with a few keystrokes. It's humanizing and it's liberating because there are no secrets. It's transparent, it's virtuous— and technology has taken us there because your unhappy customer can use it to lay waste to the bull; speed of resolution is imperative!

And how do consumers put it to use? Well, if a company really makes them angry, they create a website called www.yourcompany-sucks.com and tell the world that your company is dishonest and despicable and your products and/or service are even worse. They make a video rant and post it on YouTube, and it goes viral. A lot of companies have taken the approach of hiring resources that do nothing but monitor the Internet, specifically social media, and respond to tweets, emails, postings, and blogs, but this has proven to be an ineffective strategy. It's better to put that effort into not making the mistakes in the first place than to try and defend why the mistake was okay or is to be expected in the course of business. The consumer doesn't care that you have 25 million customers; as far as she's concerned, it's a one-on-one relationship. This is where executives in big corporations lose track of what's on the ground.

There is a lot of money spent by corporations on trying to get these attack blogs taken down, but approaching it this way invariably blows up in their faces, because somebody finds out that the big bad corporation tried to take Mary's blog down because she said mean stuff about them, and then the problem gets ten times worse. The media outlets love to grab onto that type of story and characterize, "Look, it's the big, nasty corporation." In this case the company is in fact the big, nasty corporation, right? So the company is stuck playing defense, and defense is a losing position to take if you're trying to gain market share.

Companies cannot defend or cut their way to prosperity. They need to just be a bit better every day. Spend the money on getting better, spend the company resources on getting better, and spend calories on getting better. Change the company mind-set. It's not about hushing the outcry of customers who believe, rightly or wrongly, that they have been victimized. Granted, there certainly are people who just complain about everything, and there's a prevailing wind at the executive level to say, "We're just going to categorize all complainers into that bucket," a school of thought that says, "I couldn't make them happy if I gave them my products and services for free." And the company would be right about some of them, but that's not reality with respect to the lion's share of customers.

Companies have the right to have a good enough relationship with customers to know whom they can or cannot satisfy. They have the right not to do business with people who are unreasonable. Companies do *not* have the right to assume that everybody is unreasonable and that they should just accept whatever is given to them. If the assumption going in is that "the customers are stupid and they should take what I give them," then the company is probably going to get what it deserves, which is disdain from customers. The customers may express their disdain by starting that blog or taking their complaints to consumer advocate sites such as The Consumerist, where anyone can air their grievances to the world. It is a great example of the frustration that consumers feel when they are helpless against the nameless, faceless corporations. The company can then be dismissive and say, "Well, these people are crazy and unreasonable. Therefore, their complaints are without merit."

But is the essence of what complainers are talking about, true? Is the company mistreating them? In many cases, the answer is yes. A more proactive approach by the business should be around some kind of change effort, which is led by the analysis in search of the root cause of a customer's frustration and admitting there might be a problem and some merit to what they are saying, then putting resources into fixing that stuff. Executives can't hoard information anymore. They can't hide performance anymore—just ask Bernie Madoff or any politician. Eventually, it all comes out. It comes out much sooner, and it gets distributed much more widely because of the information technology, i.e., the Internet that we know, love, and must deal with.

Some companies have seen the light and have embraced it. I mentioned Amazon earlier and how allowing—in fact, encouraging—customers to variously praise or vent about products on their site was a proactive, smart way to market. Good, bad, or indifferent, users are allowed to sort reviews; they can even mark whether they believe a review or not, they can ask the reviewer a question, and the business providing the goods can comment. There's a great example of a company proactively embracing the online medium. The culture of a business needs to be pointed toward embracing the available technology, embracing the world being flat, acknowledging where a company may come up short while getting transparent and vulnerable with the customer. However, business was not traditionally designed to work that way.

Look at companies that are vulnerable and transparent, the ones that come to mind are those familiar names that business writers use all the time as examples: Zappos and Southwest Airlines. Both have the reputations of being very transparent, and that comes from the leadership.

Southwest's example is particularly telling because the airline industry is highly competitive, price sensitive, and commoditized and has gone through great turmoil from external factors over which they have little control, such as fuel prices and labor union demands. The playing field between airline companies is probably about as level as it gets, yet Southwest has been able to turn a profit every year since their inception. So what does that say? Is it that they just have people who are super-human and exceptionally smart, or do they have a system that is based on a culture everybody understands, accepts, and agrees with, while also knowing what market they are serving?

They know what they can deliver to their customers, and they know what they can't deliver to their customers, so they make sure they don't overpromise. They always overdeliver, and when they make a mistake, they admit it, or they tell you that their service is not for you and that you should seek another vendor. That is as vulnerable and transparent as a company can get. Herb Kelleher once got a letter from a passenger who didn't appreciate the colloquial joking way in which the flight attendants delivered the

safety demonstration. Kelleher replied simply, "We will miss you."[1]
He stood behind his people; he stayed true to his mission demon-
strating transparency, and vulnerability (see fig. 3). They take safety
seriously, but they don't take themselves too seriously. He was willing
to say that to a customer and admit that his company might not
be right for them. The assumption by corporations or companies to
think that they are right for everyone is incredibly arrogant when you
think about it. How could they possibly believe that everybody needs
their product? That's a ridiculous assertion. You can't be everything to
everybody, so why are you trying?

Figure 3

These textbook examples are all taught in business school. You
know the mantra—"Customer first, customer first, dependability,
create a culture that people want to work in and make it work for
customers," but not everybody seems to be able to accept it or find a
way to apply those lessons to their own business. Why not, since we
all know it is true?

---

1 Patrick Lencioni, *The Advantage: Why Organizational Health Trumps Everything Else in Business* (San Francisco, Jossey-Bass, 2012).

The thing is, simple ideas are hard to adopt and deploy. The old cliché says, "Work smarter, not harder." We all say it, but we don't really think it, and we definitely don't act it. It is why the simple notion of the virtual workforce has taken decades to deploy, and even now when it's done, it's not done right. There are many companies that have tried virtual workforces and failed. Why hasn't it worked? The manager might say, "It doesn't work because I'm not here to see you working." Wrong. It's because you have not communicated a good mission and vision to your employees who, as a result, do not feel any connectivity. If you cannot do that with your employees, you certainly cannot do that with your customers.

You're saying to yourself, "Okay, let's say we buy all this. This mess is so big, so deep, and so tall. How are we going to tackle this?"

The way to do it is business jiu-jitsu; work with what you have. Accept what you have, change what you can, and be more patient than you think you can stand. Break the workflow and the company processes down into the silos that are creating the problems (I mean, opportunities!), and eliminate the issues, one silo at a time. How do you eat an elephant? One bite at a time.

CHAPTER 4

EATING THE ELEPHANT

Some ideas on how to make it possible.

The reality, I believe, is that all change starts small. The big picture is just too unwieldy, too incomprehensible, and seemingly immovable. But give us something individual, quantifiable, and personalize-able and, suddenly, our perspective shifts to the one.
—Mick Ebeling

The lack of communication between silos is the root of most problems and inefficiencies. Add to that the complicating factors of turf wars and politics, as elaborated by Patrick Lencioni, in his book *Silo's, Politics, and Turf Wars*, which inevitably occur when you pour the human condition into the bucket (which is really what a silo is—a bucket representing a "department" or business unit).

Full disclosure: I used to love buckets and bucketizing. "Bucketize"—it's not even a word. What does it mean? We sort things into different buckets, which we call silos. Silos break down complex systems and make them simple; they allow management to idiot-proof the system (see fig. 4). *Get creativity outta here—you don't need no stinkin' creativity. You do not need to think. You're not here to think. You're here to sort things (i.e., activities) into the buckets. Carry this bucket of completed work to the next step in the process.* The intention is to create repeatability and measurability. But what it really creates is isolation, desperation, and inefficiency, because it stops the flywheel of change and isolates segments of the workflow that create speed bumps for the otherwise smooth flow of work from intention to retention. Bucketizing assumes that by breaking the customer experience into separate components, the experience will be handled in a way that enables accountability and measurement ... from the command and control perspective of traditional management.

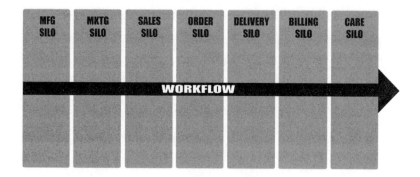

Figure 4

It is true that while the customer's experience (i.e., the bouncing ball moving through the workflow) is in a particular silo, you want to optimally handle that specific interaction. The issue comes when the ball bounces to the next silo, and the actions that have been taken to augment the customer experience are myopically focused only on that particular sequence and do not pay respects to either the outgoing product—the next task in the sequence—or the incoming product, representing the current level of customer experience.

For example, when the customer hops from the marketing silo into the sales silo, marketing may have told the customer everything they wanted to hear. When you look at that, you might say, "That's what Marketing is supposed to do"—but not if Sales can't deliver. It does not help the relationship with the customer to set unrealistic expectations. It makes it appear that the company—not just marketing—has not been honest with the customer.

It also doesn't help to push the problem forward. Sally in customer service says, "I'm going to transfer you to another department, because your issue is really special and you need to go to the special issues department."

"Thank you, Sally, for getting me to the right person."

And where does Sally send you? If you are lucky, you are not simply disconnected. And if you are, that's not necessarily Sally's fault; it's something in the workflow. You then land in the "special" silo where another person, who isn't quite as chipper and willing to help, takes over. Your expectation has been set incorrectly, assuming Sally even sent you to the right place—but that's a whole different part of the discussion. The point is the inattention to the fact that you, the customer, *and your experience* will go to the next silo (see fig. 5).

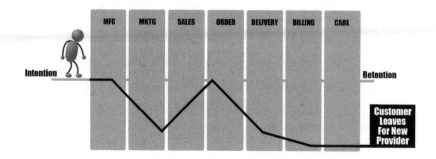

Figure 5

If you work across silos, you know the phrase "pass the trash," because silos in large companies simply pass the trash. Most of the time, it is not nefarious; there is simply a lack of understanding concerning what will occur in the next phase. The employees just know that they're out of options and after all, "It's not my job; my work is done here, so I'm going to send you over to my supervisor."

But the supervisor does not have all the information. Maybe the customer service rep didn't collect all of the relevant information, and when the customer lands in the next silo, they have to start over. How many times have you called the bank and been transferred around and had to give the same information over and over again? Personally, I'm to the point now where I can call the bank and answer their questions before they ever ask—I know the sequencing of the authentication process that well. I don't mean punching in the numbers on the handset; I'm talking about when I am speaking to a human being. The fact that they collect information with the Interactive Voice Response (IVR) system first and then validate it, may be even more annoying. Why didn't they do it the first time? "Well, that was a different department." Those are typical silo issues—process issues within the silo—that are compounded when moving from one silo to another.

As the customer's issue is getting "triaged," the company is abusing the customer and damaging the experience. Maybe it is just a little poke at each step from the different silos, but it is definitely a thousand cuts—and that is where the overall customer experience degrades. There is a lot of attention being paid to certain phases of the customer experience. Some companies would like to believe that customer experience starts and ends with any single interaction between customer and agent on the phone, but we must remember it was the customer's anger or dissatisfaction that probably prompted the call in the first place. That is why the call center typically starts behind the 8 Ball and on the defensive. As the call center rep, you are not the person who shipped the defective product, but you are the one taking the heat from the angry customer. So what do you do? You want to just push it on to the next silo, and that is what the system is set up to allow for—"I'm not authorized to make those changes, so I'll just pass the trash."

In the name of structuring consistency, companies tend to over-idiot-proof, rather than spending the money and the time on training and trust building with a workforce that is creative and wants to use their brains. What's needed is a new paradigm of interaction;—one in which the workforce is empowered to make some decisions and work through a problem to resolution. Instead we bucketize every-thing into silos, and we don't pay attention to the SIPOC (suppliers, inputs, process, outputs, and internal customers) and how the external customer's journey is affected.

THE SEVEN THINGS WE DO TO A CUSTOMER—GOOD AND BAD

What is intention to retention? Intention is the beginning of the sales cycle, in its purest form. It is the entrepreneurial light bulb of innovation—the moment where a company decides that they are going to provide some kind of product or service to some kind of customer. At that point, that customer is unaware of the existence of this product or service, even if it's a "me too" product. As a prospect, she is firmly on the "line of ambivalence"; this is the point of inception, the prospect has no opinion about the product or service. She neither loves nor hates this product or its supplier because she does not know it exists. So that is where we start, assume it is a new company and not a product line extension—it is a clean slate.

Moving forward from intention, we arrive at the first silo, which is manufacturing; in a product life cycle, that would be where we decide what color it is going to be and what it is going to be made out of, and we complete the assembly and packaging process. There is a whole set of subtasks that must occur: Focus groups, market testing, and tasks to determine who the customer will be and how much she will want to pay. But the end result is a product ... and a price ... and a package ... and a feature ... and a benefit that the product or service represents. There are some external or "end customers" impacted during this phase. The company is theoretically reaching out and touching someone, so there is some awareness outside of the company's product vision.

A good example of this is Apple. They have little skunkworks teams working on new products, and they very judiciously leak things to the public to create intrigue about what Apple will announce in the near future. There is a whole industry built around trying to figure out what the next Apple product to hit the market will be, based on what parts Apple is ordering from Asia. There were people speculating on the Apple Watch two years before it ever was announced. Apple has at least some control over this. They understand this concept because they use this as a form of "dry" test marketing. They want to see, "What's going on? Are they going to like it? Are they going to love it? How much will they pay for it? What's the buzz going to be?" The whole manufacturing phase has customer impact, and it will move the early adopter segment of the target market above or below the line of ambivalence—maybe only fractionally, but there is some movement. How curious were you about the Apple Watch before it actually appeared? Certainly if you're an Apple devotee, you knew about it. You had an opinion about it and probably had questions like, "Is it going to be cool? How much is it going to cost? Would I like one? Is it going to be Bluetooth? Is it going to have a phone in it?" You hadn't seen the darn thing, because it didn't exist yet, but you had an impression—and companies are responsible for that. During the construction phase, the people inside the manufacturing silo are responsible for maintaining the customer experience, hopefully above the line of ambivalence. They should at least be aware of it.

The next silo after construction is marketing. What does marketing do? Well, everyone thinks they know what marketing does; marketing talks us into buying stuff we don't want or need. Actually, marketing is responsible for the overall branding. During branding, the whole intention is to raise the product or service as far above the line of ambivalence as possible.

But there are some marketing tactics that are a little bit exasperating, like telemarketing, direct mail, and door hangers. Do they work? Yep, they work. Are they annoying? I think even telemarketers themselves will tell you it's annoying when it happens to them, especially in the middle of dinner. In this silo, something happens, and it's always something that is taking the product that construction or manufacturing has created in its role as supplier to marketing. That's what the "S" in SIPOC stands for—supplier. Construction, a.k.a. manufacturing, says to marketing, "Here it is. It's blue. It's 6 feet tall, and it costs $12.99. Go."

Breaking down the internal workflow into silos is common; however, breaking down the silo is less universal, and even more uncommon is examining how an internal process may affect the next silo in the workflow. Enter the SIPOC concept, where S stands for supplier, I for input, P for process, O for output, and C for customer (see fig. 7). There is a SIPOC breakdown for each silo or department within a company workflow. The concept of "customer" being the next silo in the workflow is somewhat new, although congruent with company goals of thinking "customer" first. In this case, it's the internal customer, but I believe the external customer will benefit from higher quality and service at each step in the workflow, too. This concept doesn't come as naturally as the company's "think customers first" initiative, when focused on the internal as opposed to the external customer. We already know that improving the external customer experience is hard. It's even harder to think about an internal peer group as customers, but that's what needs to happen for overall lasting external improvement.

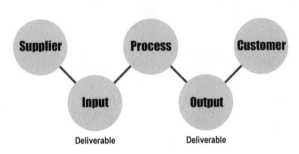

Figure 7

Everything we've talked about with respect to the external customer's journey relates to the SIPOC model and its impact *within* the silos. It's a microcosm of the same idea, which is, "Within my silo, I want to think about intention to retention," albeit a smaller scale of the process. Within the silo, I intend to do something with whatever my supplier has handed me, and I'm going to deliver that to a customer—in this case, assuming I'm in the middle of the workflow, to the next silo. If it works internally, it works externally. That's why I talk a lot about company culture; you need to learn, live, love, and apply the term "customer" inwardly as well as externally.

The second silo in the illustration is Marketing, which goes out and starts testing things and making impressions in the market. And they might get some feedback, so they might come back and say, "We need it in pink, and it needs to be half the size; and we think we can charge $27 for it." During this phase, there is interaction with the target customer group. And, once again, the customer moves somewhere above or below the line of ambivalence (see fig. 8).

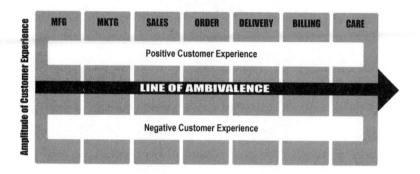

Figure 8

The whole concept of the line of ambivalence and the customer's journey through the silos is that you don't always get to start at zero or *on* the line of ambivalence in every silo. You start at the point where the previous silo left the customer, and you are forced to deal with the customer in the condition created by the previous silo. So if I have a positive experience because I've been hearing about this cool Apple Watch, then I'm above the line of ambivalence. But if the ads insult my intelligence or offend me, I'm going to fall below the line of ambivalence when I transition to the sales silo. Of course, it is possible to lose the prospect at any point during their journey from intention to retention—a company representative working with the prospect in any silo may make such a big mistake that the prospect withdraws—without giving the company a chance to recover. In some call center's metrics, these appear as "abandoned calls."

Marketing prepares the offer, pricing, and packaging and tells sales, "We're giving you air cover with our best market advertising; here are your ad sheets and your brochures and stuff. Go sell." Sales people go out to the marketplace and identify an opportunity and they get the customer in the condition in which she was left by marketing—somewhere above or below the line of ambivalence. Whether the prospect is above or below the line of ambivalence should shape the focus of the sales department. Salespeople cannot assume the customer is *on*, or always above, the line of ambivalence, although that is often done in sales. And when the sale doesn't close, what does the sales department do? They recognize the line of ambivalence and start the blame process; "The marketing was poor. That's why we didn't make the deal." Humans are good at throwing blame. Humans are not really good at saying, "You know what, marketing? The way you packaged that customer experience for me is awesome. Do more of that." There's simply not a lot of that going on.

Why? Because there's no communication between marketing and sales. Why not? They are not incentivized that way. They are incentivized to do a good job with marketing, but they are not typically incentivized on how well they transfer the lead to the sales department.

Back to the example—now the customer is interacting with the sales team. The salespeople are going to do something to the customer; they are going to try and sell her. It's easier to talk about negative examples, so let's talk about the "classic" car dealer. The customer has heard about the new car that's coming out, she saw the commercial, and it looks awesome. So she goes down to the car lot with high expectations, anticipating a beautiful customer experience—and she meets the car sales equivalent of Herb Tarlek (Google Tarlek WKRP) in his plaid jacket, and he is going to cram her in the car. She is definitely somewhere far below the line of ambivalence by the time Herb gets done. Say she actually gets through the experience, and Herb is successful in his efforts to cram her into the car. Where does she go next? Typically, she moves to some version of a delivery silo.

In the car example, the customer will eventually deal with the employees who are going to shine the car up and get it ready. Maybe they do a fabulous job and they're very attentive and even apologetic about the way the customer was treated by the salesperson. This is the service and delivery piece. Now, there's some scheduling as part of service and delivery; the car as ordered may not be in stock, but it's going to be in soon. The customer has got to come back in a week to complete the delivery process.

In telephony, cable, and utilities, a customer schedules an appointment, and scheduling is another call center function—and that's an opportunity for the company to exceed expectations or screw up big time. Then there is a routing and dispatch function, and there is the technician actually showing up at the door. The silos, or departments across the company workflow, affect the customer's journey while acting as both supplier and customer to one another in the creation of the customer experience.

In summary, the customer moves from construction, to marketing, to sales, to order intake, to service and delivery, to billing (see Fig. 8). How is the customer going to pay for the goods? Sticking with the car example, the customer gets the financing coupon book in the mail—or maybe they don't get the coupon book, so they don't know whom to pay. Oddly, even if the finance company can't seem to get the customer the materials to pay, the collection agents can certainly find the customer to tell them they haven't paid and that they are late. And there are going to be additional fees and threats because the company going to "come get the car while they are at work." That's the billing function—internally, billing is the customer of the service and delivery department.

After billing, assuming billing is complete, the company has customer care functions. The customer may not know how to work the radio. The customer says things like, "What is satellite radio? How do I find my pay-per-view? Where is the closest ATM to me?" It doesn't matter what the industry is; this is what happens to the customer in any business. There are essentially seven silos to work through—this creates the customer journey (see Fig. 8).

After customer care or education, the next thing in the workflow is "new and improved product sales time." The company has a new and improved product or service that the customer has already bought, or the company has an additional product or service. So is it easier to sell a person who is above or below the line of ambivalence? Everybody together! "Well, it's much easier to sell to somebody who's satisfied than it is somebody who is angry or sitting *on* the line of ambivalence."

That is the life cycle of the customer from intention to retention. If the company has the customer above the line of ambivalence, then it is easier to sell them more. In fact, it is six times more profitable to sell to an existing customer than it is to sell a new customer. If you (as the reader) haven't believed me up to this point, please believe me now, because depending on which study you read, the acquisition of a new customer is 5 to 25 times more expensive than keeping an established one.[2] That's SIPOC; that's intention to retention. Figure 9, illustrates the goal of the customer journey.

---

2 Amy Gallo, *The Value of Keeping The Right Customers*, Harvard Business Review, October 29, 2014.

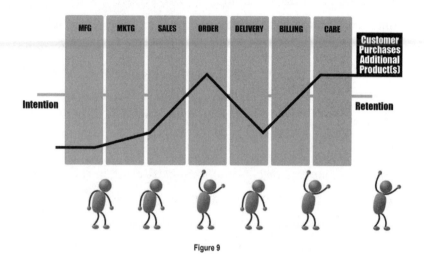

Figure 9

The bugaboo in all of this is that when companies are created as monopolies (think the Hated 5), their back office systems are built for efficiency, not for customer care or customer experience. They are built to move stuff through the system (read workflow through silos) at the lowest possible cost and without respect to the fact that it is really more valuable to have a customer above the line of ambivalence so the company can sell more. Why? Because a monopoly doesn't give a darn about that—customers can't buy what a monopoly is selling anywhere else. If I am the electric company, why would I care about the customer's experience? "Sit in the dark if you don't like it. You're going to buy it from me or ... me. How does that sound?"

Does the company build additional costs related to customer service into the system if they are a monopoly? No. Why would they do that? That would be idiotic. Thus, the process and systems, over the course of maturation of business from the industrial revolution into the Internet age, have been difficult for monopolies because their foundational DNA, attitude, and cultures were not predicated on providing any level of real "customer service."

This is why so many of them, I believe, are under attack from mom-and-pop small business startups. Small companies can take market share from big companies simply because they provide great customer service. So how important is it? Insert "David and Goliath" or whatever metaphor you want to use—it is life and death.

OKAY, NOW WE'RE CONVINCED THAT WE NEED TO EAT THE ELEPHANT.

We understand why it's important. We believe that it would be a fruitful pursuit to adjust our thinking. How do we begin?

Your first step is to find the courage to make a small change—anywhere, in any silo, usually in the place that is hurting the most. You must find the silo that is underperforming by everybody's estimation and review, making it irrefutable that this particular silo needs help. It is usually the one that everybody blames for any bad things that happen in the company.

In cable, it's popular to blame the field operations; they blame the technician who showed up late in a truck that didn't have the right tools or the right equipment or the right training. It is the field's fault. Okay—but is it *all* the field's fault? Based on intention to retention and the silos, I think it is clear that the technician did not get to the customer's door with the intention of not knowing what he was doing or how to do it or not having the necessary materials. An entire infrastructure upstream from that event contributed, in some way, to the failure of that part of the operation.

The suggestion here for the "undercover boss" reading this book is to find who is hurting the most—the silo that everybody blames. Then, go put your arm around them, and apply the SIPOC (Supplier, Input, Process, Output, Customer) analysis within that silo. Look at the supplier and the customer of that particular silo and work backward/upstream and forward/downstream in the workflow to ensure that the customer experience improves. *Do not* look to find the one person or department within that silo who is screwing up; look at processes and tools first. If you are in that silo and not at the Executive or C-Level, speak up and better yet, be first to do so.

The question is, how can you be more transparent as far as the customer's experience is concerned? How do you get vulnerable? Take a good, hard look in the mirror and say, "Gee, I could do this better, because if I did, the next silo could do their job better."

Then have a conversation with your internal supplier and say, "Hey, if you could do this particular thing differently, we could do our job better." You may find that you have to jump three or four silos back up the chain, depending on where you start. Typically, the department that habitually gets the blame in any customer experience or any workflow situation is the department that interacts directly with the customer. This is the "dramshop rule" of customer service—like a bartender who is held responsible for a patron's actions after leaving the drinking establishment, you serviced them last, so you own the outcome. It is the bank teller who takes all the blame, when in reality, it is the companies back office policy that is the problem. The teller has the unfortunate job of delivering the product and shouldering the responsibility. Everybody else at the company goes home feeling good about themselves, because they have somebody to blame. But they are not looking at their own part in the debacle.

Depending on where you are in your organization, you want to look as far up and down the workflow as you can from your vantage point and put yourself in those other silos and start a conversation with them. I don't mean an accusatory conversation; I mean asking them, "Why do you do this this way?" because they may have a very good reason.

The company must look at the workflow holistically, because that is the way the customer is looking at it. The customer's opinion of the company as a whole is only as good as his last experience with whatever silo he was in. The experience can get tainted or tweaked or shaded a little bit, as there are multiple interactions.

Do not first look to find the one person or department within that silo who is screwing up; look first at processes and tools used by the people within the department.

I have been a customer of Sprint since they were Nextel. I finally have had enough, and I'm dangerously close to leaving after 15 years. When I think about them, I do not think about the five or six years that I was a maven for them. I think about the last several years when they apparently stopped reaching across silos and approaching customer service holistically—or providing no customer service at all. The first ten years of the relationship were awesome; now I dislike them. As they got worse, they became very good at one thing, and that was convincing people who called in for service to rank them high on the customer service survey that they received shortly after their call. In essence, it was all about the rankings and not about solving clients' problems. Sprint is number one in convincing customers to score them high, even when they do not fix a customer's problem. They are awesome at it. Talk about eating the elephant—this is ignoring the elephant and eating a bowl of sugar instead.

Recently, I had a Sprint customer service representative begin crying because I was honest with her and I said, no, I could not rank her high, because she hadn't done anything. She tried, but my problem remained, and there was no solution. And it wasn't her fault; it was something upstream from her. But I couldn't say that everything was peachy keen, because it wasn't. She started crying and telling me that she couldn't get another bad review or she was going to lose her job. Of course, I felt bad and gave her a good review. The point is that she spent twice as much time begging me to give her a good review as she spent telling me she couldn't help me.

So now that we understand the problem; the question becomes, how do we overcome the ingrained reluctance to reach across the silo wall to the guy in the next silo, rather than falling back in the bunker mentality of hunkering down and covering your butt?

CHAPTER 5

WHERE THE RUBBER
MEETS THE ROAD

How to take (and not take) action!

Many things which cannot be overcome when they stand together yield themselves up when taken little by little.
—Quintus Setorius

S tarting here, I would like to have my text speak directly to you as the reader. My intent, is to give you tactical actions for implementing the ideas behind the Change is Great philosophy; actions that can bring change regardless of your level, position, or authority in your own organization.

Where do we start the change efforts to fix the processes? First, we have to identify the problem with some analysis—careful, considerate, objective, dispassionate analysis. The only way to accomplish this is to be self-reflective; avoid reflexively and aggressively going after your internal supplier on the front end or your internal customer on the back end. Most everyone in any company is accustomed to working within their silo or department and looking for efficiencies within their area. You will rarely find that managers and operational people are looking for efficiencies that relate to their internal supplier or internal customer—the departments on either side of their silo. They are not typically attuned to how the particular processes within their silo or department impact the end result. In other words, mangers within a silo are simply looking to drive out costs or to make things move faster within their own particular purview.

Only after examination of intention to retention within one silo will you have any chance to understand how you might change the activities within a specific silo and determine appropriate suggestions for you—the internal supplier or customer. This is the point at which an outside consultant may be useful to you. An outside consultant is not deterred by politics and agenda and is able to democratically and sympathetically look at the SIPOC (Supplier, Input, Process, Output, Customer) within each silo and communicate ideas in a nonthreatening way. The problem in proceeding without outside assistance is that as soon as you confront somebody in another silo about what they are doing, they are going to get defensive. It is just a natural human reaction. I'm not saying it is impossible to do without an outside consultant, but it does require a little more creativity and a willingness to slow down to spend time building a relationship and a decent level of trust. Otherwise, your efforts will be counterproductive, and you just put the other silo on the defensive.

A consultant is not the magic pill; any time a consultant comes in, some people will automatically get defensive. Typically, when there's a consultant hired, it is interpreted to mean that someone higher up in the company believes there is a need for change, and obviously they are serious about it because they have brought help in from outside. That is a bit threatening, but if you hire the right consultant, it won't be (see Chapter 10).

The next step is to engage in a purposeful conversation with clearly outlined goals for the betterment of everyone, meaning the company in general, which will also impact the company's external customers. Next, conduct an analysis of all stakeholders in the target silo. This is where a consultant can come in to assess, in a nonjudgmental way, the stakeholder group and see who is going to be receptive, who is going to be protective or defensive, and who is going to be an obstructionist.

It has often been observed that there are three levels of personality types: those that watch things happen, those that make things happen, and those who wonder what's happening. This last group doesn't seek to understand what's going on but will do their best to shut everything down because they don't like change. They don't spend the time to evaluate whether it is good, bad, or indifferent. The attitude is, "That's how we've always done it." Everybody will deny they ever had that thought, but they're kidding themselves. It is just basic human nature—"new and different" is scary.

Pick your partners and your battles: Who is going to be easiest to work with? It is not usually who you think. If you are doing this internally, you might assume, "I've known Lynne over in my supplier silo for a long time. We've gone to conferences, and we have a good relationship." That might be a good place to start, but do not assume this new interaction will be more fruitful because of that relationship. The change effort may require less of a social awareness of one another and more business respect. Successful change also recognizes congruence around the idea of change for the betterment of the two silos and, ultimately, the external customer. If you can find the later, professional alignment, as well as personal alignment, you can make magic; we have all been on or seen what a great team can accomplish—regardless of talent.

Once you understand what you're going after, where you're going, and you've analyzed the human factors within the other silo, you need to approach and set out some goals, including timelines and objectives. You need to be flexible enough to know that as things change, there will be necessary adjustments to the strategy and frequent communication of the changes. The most important thing is to get started; do not become paralyzed by the analysis process. Frequently, companies call a consultant after attempting a change effort themselves—because they can get derailed during the analysis phase. This happens when ideas floated as trial balloons during the discovery analysis get shot right out of the air. The effort loses steam and momentum. It's just easier to let the *status quo* survive. When you use an external consultant, it shows you are motivated to avoid this trap and keep the project moving.

Another important reason to use external consultants is that they are hired to accomplish a specific outcome, which in this case is change. It's difficult when you try to address change internally, chances are good that you don't have extra cycles (or spare time) during a day. Almost every employee in every industry has been forced to "do more with less" over the past two decades. Instead, new projects are just another added responsibility as part of ongoing business and as a member of that particular silo. I don't know a lot of companies that are overstaffed to the level where they can inject a major project pursuing a global cultural change on top of the normal day-to-day obligations of the business.

If you are going to do it internally, then you need to empower somebody with the tools and the time that it is going to take to do it properly. It is not something you can accomplish during the already-busy, 40-plus-hour workweek. You must also understand that there may be issues for the person whose task suddenly becomes informing his colleagues that they are doing something the wrong way; in many situations, existing relationships will get in the way of proper communication and follow-through. A person may be tempted to pull punches or settle old scores. When this happens, as it often does, you will not get an objective analysis.

The other thing I've seen companies do is establish an internal group to "imitate" consultants, using internal people who are the equivalent of an internal affairs department. This tactic is probably the worst. Other times, a project management office will be established, usually comprised of people who run projects; therefore, they know the methodologies. Once again, the problem is that there are too many relationships in the way because the project management team is typically a service provider to all of the silos. The existing relationships and feelings will complicate things, and the change effort will not be "clean." As a result, the change effort typically stalls or gets put down by the target—because they see the change coming, and instead of supporting the effort to achieve change, they intensify their efforts to torpedo it.

As a consultant, I have encountered many situations where a company tries this approach, and the result is an epic failure. Probably the most ubiquitous example is the business group that wants to deploy a software tool. Most often, they are replacing one tool with the latest and greatest edition. They interview outside implementation teams to get the project deployed and installed. That obviously has a cost, and it looks a lot like support. The first thing the company or the impacted silo does is start advising the vendor who is selling the tool on how to implement it—"Why don't you screw this in here?"

The inherent flaw, particularly in the software business, is most tools are similar, and that is how they bring the cost down. They build a tool once and sell it many times to many different industries. Their customers use it in ways that are similar but not necessarily the same. This is the reason why many software companies have implementation partners that are tasked with attempting to bridge the gap between the somewhat generic tool and the specific instance within the vertical for which the tool is intended.

For example, in the cable business, the silo hires a company to implement another company's software to help manage their customer accounts. When that happens, there's a domain knowledge that comes along with it, and sometimes the software vendor will pay for those implementers. Ordinarily, though, it is just buried in the licensing costs. At the end of the day, regardless of which methodology is utilized, the company and the silo within the company are footing the bill. Then the silo says, "You know what? These people don't really know our business. Since our people are going to use this tool, why don't we let them implement it?" This is also known as the "let's go it alone" methodology. It sounds perfectly plausible, but the vendor company can then simply walk away from any responsibility related to the tool's adoption and use, allowing everything to fall on the people who also have to use the tool.

This is just an example of the many issues that come with change. There will be people who do not want to change. They do not want this damn new tool. They like their old tool. Why? Well, because they don't want to learn to use something new when they believe they already know what needs to be done. The combination of a weak implementation team from the standpoint of domain knowledge, combined with a resistant user base, is akin to forcing a square peg into a round hole. The typical result is an 18- to 24-month root canal process for that silo. If the tool finally gets implemented, it is not as efficient as the vendor described and does not accomplish the goals of the silo or the company. This is a rampant problem with the larger enterprise's resource planning systems. The fear of failure and resultant pushback is amplified by the threat of job loss, inherent in larger organizations.

Fear of change is truly a fear of loss, the result of misunderstanding the necessary steps to affect real change that include proper control and adoption processes, which would have been addressed by outside professionals, or passionate internal change specialists. Frequently, the fear of change is a cost-driven mistake because no one wants to pay for the planning and the time that it takes to achieve adoption. The solution must be about change that has been accepted and embraced, or a company is doing nothing more than planning to fail.

I have discussed many resistance or "fear" points: one is money, two is change itself, three is methodology, and four is the tool itself. People may not agree with the selection process and/or the selection itself. All of it boils down to human factors that haven't been properly considered and addressed during the planning stage.

At this point, many will simply circle back to the idea of brute force deployment that says, "We bought it, and management says we're using it," or, "We're turning off the old system whether you like it or not." These are just simple fixes that are typically employed. "You'll use it, and you'll love it."

"Why?"

"Because I said so."

We all know how well that works. Such a process sounds a lot like parenting because, in reality, that is exactly what it is—but without the humanization. And, just like parenting, changes can result in tantrums and hard feelings, tears, and the eventual very real possibility that some resources are going to need a time out—or an outright firing.

THE PERILS OF IDIOT-PROOFING

During a change effort, there will likely be a time where the old system, process, or tool has been canceled or turned off. This is the point of no return. Predictably, the outcome with this option is something less than desired or expected. The kneejerk response from the enterprise is to break things down in order to reduce the training time and the resistance level, as well as to increase the ability to resist the deployment. We do that by idiot-proofing systems and processes.

Under the banner of structure and efficiency, and straight from the accounting version of central casting, we get the documentation experts who come in and write something that *looks* like methods and procedures. The sentiment behind all this work is, "Just do it this way, idiot." Most of the time we leave the "idiot" off at the end of the sentence, but you can still hear it: "Your job is not to think. Your job is to follow this path, these breadcrumbs we've thoughtfully left for you. Just do it this way. There's no need to do it any other way. There's no need to inject your personality or your thought process. What we need you to do is to do it this way. Every time—1, 2, 3, A, B, C—follow the model."

This is where the wheels really come off because what you've done when you hand employees a document like this is dehumanize the system to the point where the resources (your people) that live in that environment are not motivated to do anything but follow the model. But since they are dealing with other human beings on the other end of the process, you have a major disconnect with respect to empathy and caring. If a company does not empathize with or care about the customer, then how deep is that relationship? I would submit that it is only superficial.

To complete the travesty, we expect—in fact, we demand—that the internal people behave robotically, because that makes management believe that they have control over the human beings in the system. In fact, they do, because you will see that noncompliance begets negative consequences.

If you are successful in idiot-proofing your systems, then you end up beating the creativity and caring out of your organization. That is the true definition of idiot-proofing. We want to make sure nobody gives a darn about the customer. All we want is for them to deliver services and do it our way. It is an inflexible position; it is not scalable, and it is really not tolerable in the information age, where people know things, expect to be heard, and can complete their own investigation. When the customer finally connects with a human being and that human being is no more helpful than the FAQ page of the website, it further deteriorates the customer experience and may be the final straw that results in the customer falling so far below the line of ambivalence they are lost for good. In short, idiot-proofing is not helpful, but it is the way that interactions are designed to work in silos—especially in the call center silo: "Just follow the model."

This process is likely driven by the admirable goal of driving down costs, which ultimately does help the customer. However, the process is shortsighted, because it doesn't achieve the desired result. It may reduce costs, but it also drives down humanization, and in the long run, the company pays for this, probably with its existence. You cannot cut your way to prosperity.

Many call center agents are given screens displaying scripts to read that are usually quite sophisticated. The company spends a lot of time writing and getting input from sales and marketing people, and even human factors experts, who design the flow of the logic and the words that the customer service representatives utilize when handling a phone inquiry. The goal is to reduce the operating costs of the call center. The desire is to pay minimum wage and not have to spend time training people.

Typically, there are three tiers of customer service. Tier one occurs when the phone rings and the IVR (Interactive Voice Response system) does the triage. The system relies on the customer to identify the issue they are calling about. Following the automated issue identification, the call is routed to a human representative who has been fed a series of screens based on the input from the customer. This is the minimum-wage employee who is encouraged to just read the script on the screen.

Assuming that the customer input everything correctly into the IVR and was not completely frustrated by that process, the representative on the phone reads the script on the screen that is displayed as a result of the customer's input. The likelihood that the correct screen/script comes up for the representative to read is dependent on the accuracy and intelligence around the decoding of the customer's input during the triage process. A good system will provide the representative with the correct screen/script about 80 percent of the time. Of course, this means that 20 percent of customer calls are usually handled by your lowest-paid employees, who are not even provided with the correct information to address the reason for the call.

A truly frustrated customer will demand to speak to a supervisor. Anyone who has ever called a company and been routed to a call center has learned to make this demand early on in their interaction with the Tier one representative. "Get me to your supervisor," is the colloquial term for, "Get me to Tier two." Most representatives in a call center are Tier one, and they are "prepared" to assist the 80 percent of the customers calling with an issue that the knowledge base is set up to handle. You might believe that only 20 percent of callers demanding Tier two assistance equates to success: after all, if 80 percent of the callers achieve their purpose at Tier one, things must be going in the right direction. This is wrong; instead, 20 percent of your customers calling for assistance are now falling below the line of ambivalence. The customer is now annoyed, and the Tier one representatives do not feel good because they are failing 20 percent of the time. That is how they are evaluated—if they had to transfer someone to Tier two, the call was a failure: "You didn't read the screens correctly—you are worthless."

Management never comes in and says, "Maybe the information we gave you wasn't very good." No, they just say, "You're a lousy employee. We need to find somebody else, someone that can do the job." It is dehumanizing, and who wants to put up with that? The people that will put up with a process that creates failure probably started with low self-esteem. We're going from bad to worse with respect to humanization.

Let's look at the Tier two representatives. Tier two is usually comprised of those employees who, despite a process prone to failure, were able to succeed in Tier one. They are not any more sophisticated. They are the same lowest-paid employees. They simply were able to do well within the idiot-proof system. Does that mean they're smarter, or are they just good at being … idiots? I can't answer that question, but I submit that you are beating the daylights out of any potential creativity by finding and promoting those who excel within a flawed system.

Nonetheless, the customer has arrived at Tier two, speaking to a supervisor who probably lords over 8 to 12 frontline Tier one people. What does a supervisor do? Just like Tier one, they read a script. She has a little more flexibility to make decisions but is essentially working from the same information. Now, why does she have more flexibility and a little broader power? Well, having analyzed human behavior and data from call centers, we know, that ultimately, it is possible to wear down the customer.

Is this really what we're trying to do—just wear down the customer—or are we trying to solve problems? In this current situation, what we're actually trying to do is just get them off the phone. Why? Because we don't care! We don't have empathy for the customer. We're not set up for empathy but rather for efficiency and low cost; put another way, we're set up for efficient dehumanization of the relationship with our customers. You may have heard the saying, "If it wasn't for the customers, this would be a great business!" Of course, without the customers, there is no business.

Many customers have learned they need to get to Tier three, and they know it takes a lot of intestinal fortitude to get there. How many times does a customer have to say, "Get me to your supervisor?" In Tier one, it typically takes three requests—or demands, depending on the customer's frustration level. In Tier two, it takes approximately six. By then, the customer is pretty tired and, in all likelihood, extremely frustrated. In the best of circumstances, the customer is starting to simply accept the fact that the company doesn't care. But let's say the customer is resolved to continue until they actually achieve that elusive satisfaction—achieving contact with Tier three.

Finally, the supervisor of the supervisors! However, because of the way people are promoted, this person, the last line of rule enforcers, is super-assertive and gruff. As you move up the chain, because of the design of the system, you just get less and less human. Most customers want to believe that the company actually does care, so they rationalize, "Well, they have robots on Tier one, and if you soldier on enough, you'll talk to people who really care about you." Sadly, that is not the way the customer service is designed. It is designed to move the customer around for half an hour or so, and then, after being told, "We're sorry we can't help you," they are asked to take a customer service satisfaction survey. Ironically, this is where the agent becomes the most "human."

It is hard to make the changes this system needs because change requires the stakeholders addressed earlier to acknowledge there is a problem. That is a much longer-term cultural vision issue. That is why it takes time; you have to sell it up, down, and across the organization. The examples that I have offered are all within the call center silo, but these same issues exist in every silo because everyone is striving to achieve efficiency. There is no provision made for any manner of quality. In fact, there are many lapses in quality; I am asserting that the key quality that must be applied is to the relationship with the customer. At the end of every day, the objective is to sell every customer something that will then lead them to buy something else.

The first requirement is to take a long, hard look in the mirror and say, "What does the customer see and experience, and why do we treat our customers this way?" When you take this step, you must stop at, "Well, it's going to be really expensive to spend too much time on the phone with our customer and show them we really do care about them." That is true—it is probably going to be expensive, but that doesn't mean it's not going to be profitable. If you determine there is a willingness to change the way you do things, then you can't change a piece of the culture and then continue to operate everything else the same way.

Pick up nearly any recently written book about customer service; the odds are good that you'll see Zappos offered as an example of how to do it right. What is their policy? Their customer service people are allowed to spend *as much time as it takes* on the phone with every customer. The Zappos record is more than nine hours, where a Zappos call center representative spoke with one customer for an entire shift. At the end of that, the caller didn't buy anything—but the representative was given an award by the company for keeping the conversation going for that whole shift—and he turned that caller on the other end of the phone into a customer who has spent thousands of dollars over the years following that conversation. While this is an extreme example of empathy and caring about the customer relationship, it is also indicative of the potential return on such empathy and effort.

In order to humanize its system, Zappos has employed technology in a variety of ways. They have a router that looks at the area code of every call and routes it to a call center agent from that area. That means that the conversation starts out with, "Oh, where do you live? I used to live in Wilton, Connecticut."

"Did you? What high school did you go to?"

It is brilliant. They can start a conversation—a human-scale conversation. It shows empathy and caring, and it is so simple.

What I believe they are doing here is leveraging technology to humanize the system. They are not forcing people into behaving like robots. When the screen pops up in the call center, technology identifies the originating area code, and the system looks in the employee profiles and finds an employee who is familiar with that area code. There will not be a qualified employee for every caller, but when the system does find a match, the call will always go better. If you've ever worked in a call center or been involved in any type of telemarketing, then you are aware that to know one teeny fact about the person you're talking to is an icebreaker that dramatically changes the conversation. Suddenly, the customer feels like your company actually cares. Do you really care? The customer does not know, but it certainly seems like it because you noticed enough to say, "Are you from this town or that town?" It is all about empowering your representatives with information.

> It is all about empowering your representatives with information.

In our practice, we deliver information up and down the hierarchical command structure without restriction. Giving transparency to the front line enables them to use their brains and do the right thing. Providing the knowledge and letting the representatives know they're trusted with that information empowers them to seek a relationship with the customer. Giving them access to data they can use to extract useful information is huge. It also connects them to the greater purpose of the company. It shows that the company trusts them and is invested in them.

CHAPTER 6

NEVER WEAR A FUNNY WIG

Why it's good to get close to your customer via your front line.

Outstanding leaders go out of their way to boost the self-esteem of their personnel. If people believe in themselves, it's amazing what they can accomplish.
—Sam Walton

Let's circle back to my favorite show, *Undercover Boss*. The whole premise of the show is that the disconnected C-level executive puts on a disguise, then applies for and gets a job as a frontline employee in the various departments in their large organization. Surprisingly, in every episode, the bosses come up with something brilliant as they uncover customer service issues and examples of how the company mistreats its employees. Those are just about the only two things that they come up with. There are not a lot of product ideas or innovation that comes out of it.

The show has been on for a few years. Every show is the same, yet somehow it is compelling to watch the same details play out over and over again. Employees are not treated fairly or well; employees are working around the system that has been built for them and going above and beyond, or else they are abusing customers. There is this huge lightning strike, week after week of, "Wow, our frontline people really have great ideas about how we should be dealing with our customers and how we should be treating one another." The whole idea of being open to change is that you can then actually affect change and get ideas by listening to those frontline employees.

The whole concept of *Undercover Boss* is, "Let's go get the truth." To seek the truth, you do not need to wear a disguise; rather, you need to create a culture that doesn't punish mistakes but instead celebrates trying new things and ideas that may be outside the normal course of business. Be a culture that seeks improvement as its first and foremost priority and not the repetitive idiot-proofing of processes and systems. Certainly, you need some rigor, but you don't need so much that you weed the humanity out of the systems, the processes, and the people within those frameworks.

THE PROBLEM WITH MIDDLE MANAGEMENT

As a company gets hierarchically taller, the systems and processes get perverted by middle management: the C-level suite becomes further and further disconnected from the front line as the insertion of layers in middle management pile up. Politics and insecurity can enter the system of workflow and the culture of the company. The responsibility of the C-suite is to keep this from happening, but if you are already in this situation and you are sitting here as a 40-, 50-, or 100-year-old company, then you have to accept what you have and change what you can.

Be first.

Start today.

How do you do that? The empowerment of the front line will require acceptance by middle management to allow the free flow of information. This sounds like a great and simple idea, and it is, but it is also hard to execute because you have attitudes, fears, and behaviors operating at the middle management layers that do not allow the free flow of information and empowerment of the front line. It's the reason the *Undercover Boss* structure requires wearing a disguise; because middle management would blow it up.

In most of these big companies, the CEO would not need to disguise himself to the frontline employee but would need to disguise himself so that middle management wouldn't get their defenses up. They are the proverbial monkeys in the middle, but that is their job. Their job is to push down initiatives, vision, and mission and to push up grievances and suggestions. They are the grand gatekeepers of communication, and they are the chief obstruction in the process of breaking those barriers down and getting transparency from top to bottom and bottom to top.

Yes, they do have a role, but the role, as traditionally executed, must change. The role must be that of self-worth, confidence, and trust. Upper management will celebrate mistakes and not punish (within reason, of course). Risk taking will be encouraged and not put down. That's the beginning of the culture change that must happen. Otherwise, any change effort stops at middle management.

Peer-to-peer conflict will always exist because that is competition and human nature. It is the executive's responsibility to make sure that the competition is healthy and not destructive.

From the C-suite down to the lowest levels of supervisory management, effort should be applied in the pursuit of creating systems and processes that are used by the human component, not on managing the human components. Management control should be of inanimate things, not of the people themselves. People should be self-governing within the ecosystem because the company hires the right people for the right reasons—those who understand the mission, vision, and the "why" of the company. These people operate according to the values that they bring to the table, not solely because of the rules that you have so neatly documented and enforced. Rather than putting your energies into documentation and idiot-proofing, put the energy into creating systems that offer structure without being too rigid and allow for flexibility without being too chaotic. Hitting this balance requires constant attention, which is the real role of management. That is why middle management has the most important role—and also the biggest opportunity to screw the system up.

This is where and why you get the hoarding of information. Politics, fear, vanity, and greed all drive this hoarding, but among these, fear is the biggest motivator. Fear of change—fear of what will happen and fear of getting credit or getting blamed—is why a lot of these concepts are difficult to institute. However, while you are playing defense and trying to maintain the status quo with rules and rigor, your competitors simply run right around the outside, which is why you see small upstart companies taking market share from big businesses. They are using technology, agility, and communication to reach new markets.

All you can really control is your behavior. So accept that things need to change and build a system that welcomes change, looks for change, and leverages change. We've talked about goal alignment. Middle management is responsible for the socialization of components of goal alignment. That is why it is critically important in big organizations that change efforts start with middle management.

I have a suggestion for the producers of *Undercover Boss*: A second half-hour of *Undercover Boss* should show us the same company a year later and begin with a recap of all the things the CEO asked her management team to look at and change. I would like to see the changes requested by the owner or CEO played out. What changes did they really make to their culture? They talk about changes to systems and processes, but how are they going to actually do that? Are they changing the culture, or are they simply engaging in the first half of the "Change is great, be first" theory (awareness) and then going back to the old way of making change, which is to write a memo, followed by brute force deployment?

My guess is that brute force memo writing is what most companies are doing because communication and planning change is the hard, messy part. Finding people doing stuff right and finding people doing stuff wrong is all well and good, but what do you do with that data? How do you turn it into action? How do you make them adopt? That is messy. That takes time, patience, and buy-in; you have to sell some ideas, create a culture, and get goal alignment.

In deciding where to adopt change, the front line is where the rubber meets the road. It is the bottom of the pyramid—the foundation on which your company sits. There are more employees on the front line than anywhere else, because no matter how wide the pyramid gets, there are always about ten people for every one in the next level up. Why not focus on the systems and processes that those particular individuals engage with in order to get maximum impact? It only makes sense that planning for change and crafting good communication about change is where you capture the best bang for your buck.

How does that group typically break down? The recipe, as opposed to the formula, goes as follows: The leading and lagging edges of a bell curve, sliced off at the top 15 percent, would be your employees who are going above and beyond. The 15 percent at the bottom end are the employees you cannot motivate with a cattle prod and who typically get the most attention (see fig. 10). The attention comes from solution providers—not just software providers but also consultants and management. Management spends its time dealing with the people at the top because they are fun to go to lunch with and the bottom because, in traditional organizations, they are the ones that upper management gets all the flak about. In fact, there are statistics that show that you spend 80 to 90 percent of your time on the bottom 10 percent of your employees. Why would you spend 90 percent of your time with your worst performers? Well, because they take all your time and attention, and they probably don't fit within the system that you have built. You either change the system or get rid of people.

There are all kinds of management books about differentiation. My hero, Jack Welch, has a great many thoughts on the subject, and he describes them in several of his books. Jack Welch's teaching on differentiation says that the bottom 10 percent just needs to go and needs to be moved out in a humane and sympathetic way—not in a programmatic way. My theory is based on the top and the bottom being of relative equal size. Fifteen percent of your people will figure their way out of the desert with a penknife and a battery, and 15 percent of your people don't even know they are in the desert.

That leaves us with the group in the middle—the 70 percent. This group is more than double the other two groups combined—who are largely being ignored. Why? Because they are average, and they are just doing their jobs. They are not doing spectacular work, but they aren't causing you heartburn and indigestion, either. What the "Change is great, be first" theory tells us is to focus on the top 15 percent and the middle 70 percent and to create competition between those groups. You take a good/better/best approach: you want your good in the 70 percent to become better, and you want your betters in the 15 percent to become the best (see fig. 10).

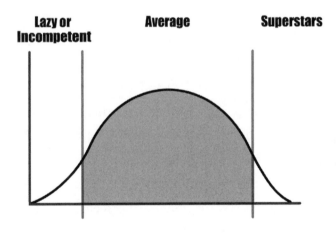

Figure 10

The idea is that we move people up through the system by adjusting the systems and the processes themselves. What we've found in our practical application is that the bottom 15 percent consists of two personality types: (1) lazy and (2) incompetent. Roughly half of those in that 15 percent are simply lazy. Lazy can be defined a lot of ways, but most of the time it is just lack of motivation, or at least they don't understand or connect with the "why" of the company, and they are there simply for a paycheck. It doesn't matter what you do to or with them, they cannot get out of the funk because they are not a good fit. Those people, while competent, don't wish to participate in change efforts or improving themselves, and they will organically leave as the 70 percent group and the upper 15 percent group begin to improve themselves. Reliably, half of the bottom 15 percent will leave because they are aware that there is change occurring and they don't want to participate. The other 7.5 percent are just incompetent. That's why you have human resources—hiring mistakes are inevitable. If there are only 7½ hiring mistakes out of every 100 people who work for you, then you are doing way better than average. In fact, you are doing way better than awesome.

You just have to accept the fact that not everybody is going to fit, and you are going to have to take some aggressive action. The idea here is not to focus our time and attention on that bottom 15 percent. It takes care of itself, or there are other mechanisms—other silos within the organization—to handle those people. What we as consultants do is provide a culture that includes systems and frameworks that facilitate the upward progression in terms of productivity of the top 15 percent and the middle 70 percent.

Here's how this has played out with our largest client. First, we accomplished getting agreement from upper management so that there would be transparency from the highest to lowest levels of frontline employees. We provided that information using technology via web tools to show information to anyone who wanted to look at it. There was very little training or oversight as to how to use the information. We simply presented performance data that related to the standard measures of productivity for field operations personnel—it was exactly what they needed.

We looked for people within the system who were doing things at or above the prescribed spec as handed down from upper management. The examination effort looks a lot like an initiative, except for the penalty phase that you see in any big organization. The idea was to reward these top ten people who are beating the desired spec on a specific, or set of specific, key performance indicators. Management recognized and applauded those people in front of the rest of their peers, and they were given a *de minimis* reward.

Within three months, we saw something magical happen; the top 15 percent got better, the middle 70 percent got better, and the bottom 15 percent moved on. Why? Because we had created healthy competition between the human components within the system; we gave them access to the numbers, we gave them access to the information—and they performed. Using their own initiative, they were able to try new things and were able to see, based on the key performance indicators that corporate was looking at, whether those changes they made had any effect on their overall performance. They could see how that related to their peers, not only in their particular area but also across the company, from coast to coast.

It turns out that people who are connected to the mission, the vision, and the purpose take the feedback and use it to become better. It didn't take middle management rolling up the report and beating people with it. It didn't take the suggestion that you need to do this or that another way. It was very, very simple. We empowered them with the information regarding the standard by which they were being judged as a group, and each person either bought into it, adjusted his behavior, or didn't.

CHAPTER 7

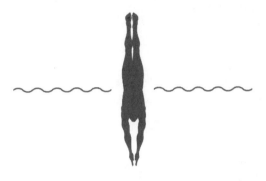

RESPECT THE FLES
(FRONTLINE EMPLOYEES)

How to get close to your frontline employees

Trust is the lubrication that makes it possible
for organizations to work.
—Warren Bennis

Now that we have determined that the front line is the logical place to start your movement toward change, how do you, a C-level executive, approach it? Our research and experience show that there is no substitute for spending time with the front line.

Get down in the dirt, into their environment, and experience what they experience. This cannot be done without either following the *Undercover Boss* method or through substantial planning and messaging. The boss cannot just show up and say, "Tell me everything that's wrong." The only people who will talk are extroverts. That will color the evaluation in a way that is going to confound the data. The boss must spend time with the FLE without asking pointed questions and must genuinely take an interest in them as human beings. Let the relationship unfold in a natural course.

Remember: these ideas will work no matter what your level in the organization!

First, build trust. Then proceed to learning. Invest the time to build the trust so that you are getting real information and not having people tell you what they think you want to hear. The *Undercover Boss* method is a little more expedient from a time standpoint because you basically get away with spying, but the blowback from that is that you have been spying on your people, which tends to degrade trust. It works well with the 15 percent at the top of the scale because they don't mind being investigated. It does not work so well with the middle 70 percent and certainly not with the bottom 15 percent, who are suspicious of management and have an "us versus them" outlook on the business relationship. You start in a hole and you just dig yourself a little deeper.

It will take time. It doesn't happen overnight. There are no quick fixes with change.

While you are building these relationships, you will see what is happening to the customer as well. It is a twofer: you are going to get firsthand experience with the customer while also getting to experience what the people who represent your brand really deal with on a day-to-day basis.

A consultant or internal project team, engaging in a frontline change project should start by with sitting down and figuring out exactly what the messaging is going to be and what the "why" is for each of the levels within the organization. How does that connect to the mission?

Our process is to we do the DNPS next, also known as "the dog and pony show." We had a project to deploy a particular piece of software across a large enterprise. Every two or three months, we'd deploy to a new city—a new market. Nobody knew what DNPS stood for, but at most large companies, the acronym thing happens quite frequently. Acronyms have become such a part of the lexicon that people don't even ask what they mean, or they are embarrassed to ask because they think they should know. This occasions some private mirth, as you might imagine. The point is do not be afraid to ask what any acronym stands for—you will find that most people don't actually know and will learn by finding out; therefore, clear communication is the root of good change.

The idea behind the DNPS meeting is to get all the levels in one room. You get the representatives you have selected to receive the messaging from the front line. These would include supporters, detractors, and naysayers. You get some middle management as well as all the executives. The meeting is run by the external project team, which is either a consulting company or a specifically delegated "special agent." It's generally an all-day affair where the overall "why" (as in why does the company exist) for the company is laid out.

The C-levels are there to talk about the project and how important it is. After about an hour or two, because they are so important and so busy, they will start getting texts and calls, and they will need to go do other things. In actuality, it is the project change team calling those executives to tell them that it is time for them to exit the room. The other people in the room see that they don't just leave—they get called away. *It is very important psychologically that it happens this way:* what they are there to do is testify and get behind the why—then they get out (see fig. 11), while the planning unfolds.

Figure 11

The reason we do this is to start opening up the door for the frontline employees and middle management to talk about the project and get their input to help design the deployment plan, because people adopt what they help create. The composition of that meeting is vital. That is why the planning must happen ahead of time—to evaluate stakeholders and the various user groups, who generally fall into one of three categories: supporters, detractors, and naysayers.

The supporters are the equivalent of what is commonly known in marketing as an early adopter. They are open to change. They like innovation, and they like to try new things. Detractors are laggards—second-wave adopters. They need a little more proof; they need to be convinced. They don't just run in and adopt things. They sit back and they see. "That new iPhone 6 looks pretty cool." Once ten of their friends have them and they say the phones are pretty cool, then they will go get one. Naysayers are the people who still carry around flip phones. They do not like change. They want the status quo. This is, unfortunately, a sizable group, because of the way our brains are wired to look for patterns and consistency. Within that group you also have a subgroup—the toxic naysayers. They are people who just like to blow things up. This is not a personality trait. This has to do with the emotional attachment to whatever is being changed. Usually, it is because they were involved with the decision to take the original route. For example, they were involved with the purchase of the software, or solution, or they designed the process in question. They are more than just a little invested for reasons beyond the company's interest. They are there for their personal interests.

If you have somebody who is emotionally involved with an effort or business process within a silo because they designed or endorsed it and that person also happens to be a laggard type of personality, that begets the perfect storm. They lie in the weeds and wait for the opportunity to shoot and blow things up. The reason they are more dangerous is because you don't know who or where they are. I can deal with laggards, with detractors, and with naysayers, because at least they are saying something. The toxic naysayers usually keep their presence hidden. They undermine efforts, and they are generally cowardly in the way they do it. They employ political means. They don't like confrontation, so they backchannel everything.

The biggest challenge to change efforts is that there is no good way to deal with these people up front because you don't know who they are until they finally pop up. You just need to be aware that these personality types exist, so you have to make plans to deal with them. In this case, the best defense is a good offense. The way to deal with toxic naysayers is to overwhelm them and expose them as early as possible. The way that you do that is through DNPS and successive status meetings where the project gets high visibility and is very inclusive. That is how you flush them out, because at some point, they are going to rear up.

Because of this phenomenon, change projects are often done with limited visibility or behind the scenes. The thinking is, "Once we have everything in place, *bam*! We'll unload it on everybody." That plays to the defense's strength, which is then to divide and conquer the group targeted for change. If you have brought the lion's share of the group along, your toxic naysayers will show themselves, and you can pick them off faster. This does not necessarily mean you get rid of them, but that certainly is an option. If you don't take steps to identify these people early on, you will not be able to deal with the problem. Surface those issues through good communication, messaging, and inclusive behaviors on the change team's part.

The change facilitation team takes on building relationships with middle management and the front line, dividing them into groups and finding where the centers of supporters, detractors, and naysayers may lie. The team must understand their platforms and the reasons for their platforms. That information leads to creation of the messaging so that you can deal with those groups. How do you leverage the supporters? How do you move the detractors? How do you eliminate the naysayers? It is all about formulating a plan and going forward with constant offensive pressure, and communication.

This is the first-third of the project; the more people involved, the longer it is going to take. People, process, and tools are the three legs of the stool. The planning and DNPS meeting take place over a period of what is usually three to five months. Then, you "create" for a month and complete the inclusive design work. Next comes a month of "deployment," followed by a month-long "bake" period, and then, finally, a month of optimization where the change team returns. Make the change. Install what you can. Let them use it for an amount of time. Then come back to optimize, tweak, and maybe add another thing or two to the change.

That's how you create the winds of change; you have a sail set up that can catch them, so you have an organization that is attuned to adjusting the sails. The bigger the organization, the more time it takes. Why? Because it is the humans that have to change. Conversion of tools and processes are the inanimate things; they have no agenda.

Let me tell you a story about myself and my company from our founding days when we were still figuring out exactly how to make this stuff work and stick. A client in Florida, called us in to consult because they were replacing the workforce automation platform through which technicians in the field received their work orders, and they needed to be sure the technicians were on board. In the preceding nearly 30 years, the dispatch manager had come in two hours before the technicians every morning and had lovingly and carefully torn apart triplicate forms from a pin feed printer and placed them in wire baskets with each technician's name on it. These forms were their job assignments for the day. Those technicians picked up four to 12 work orders, put them in their aluminum clipboard carriers, and went to their trucks with their papers and pens. That is the way it had always been—a very analog mind-set.

We came in with the intention of handing each one of those technicians a web-enabled phone. Their work orders would come down electronically via those phones; there were no wire baskets, no triplicate forms, and no beloved aluminum clipboards. Basically, this was a paperless system. All 50 of the technicians got a couple of days of training to learn how to use the phone, see the screens, address their questions, and to give them time to play with the system and get comfortable with it. We had our protocols, we had our standards, and we had our confirmation of learning and certifications. We ran parallel for about two weeks, during which they got to hold onto their beloved aluminum clipboards and their papers, while also using the new phones. And then came the day that the clipboards were taken away; as of that Sunday night, there would be no more printing work orders, no more clipboard—they just had to make sure the phone was charged.

The Friday before that full change was to happen on Monday, all the phones disappeared, as did the paper work orders. They were just gone. The technicians all came in, and they couldn't work. They all sat down in the break room and waited for instructions while they laughed their asses off because someone had taken the work orders. This was their way of making a point, which was, "We're not going to do any work whatsoever." With the way the system worked, the work orders were spooled at one o'clock in the morning and took about four hours to print. When the work orders disappeared, nobody knew that they were gone until eight o'clock in the morning. It still would take four hours to print. The jobs started at eight o'clock in the morning. Basically, by making the work orders disappear, it was impossible for the technicians to do their jobs that day. Each of these 50 techs had an average of five jobs a day.

This is what happens when you don't do change communication correctly: the frontline employees will take control, and they will ruin your business to prove a point. This illustrates how resistant to change people or an organization can be—the FLE put their jobs on the line.

What did we do wrong in this case? We did not do a good job with messaging up front. We did not identify the toxic naysayers. We let them lay in the weeds until they could strike. Obviously, it was debilitating in a big way. Over the course of a week there were potentially a couple thousand customers that couldn't be served. That's what happens when you don't do it right. Prep work was done, but it wasn't inclusive and sympathetic; we didn't have a DNPS for this deployment. A lot of the theories in this book came from that awful experience.

Now, let's go to the other side of the country—Northern California, where we had the same kind of situation. The technicians and the supervisors were involved with the plan on how and what the training would accomplish. They actually wrote some of the questions. They wrote the engagement protocols. They wrote the confirmation of learning protocols. They used a "train the trainer" model; the trainers came in and trained a certain number of key people in the market. The key people in the market trained their peers. All the technicians got their phones a week before they went into training. Many of them had figured out how to use the phones by the time that they got their own training because they were so excited about the new methodology. There was no running parallel because they got to pick the date that they cut over. The training time was cut by 90 percent.

The only thing that was different, other than my team's experience, was that we were inclusive; we spent time on the ground with them, talking to them about the system, about what their needs were and how they were different. Basically, just listening to them, involving them, and having them be part of the process of creating the new methodology, we gave them the parameters that they needed, but they got to decide how they got to those goals. We had some flexibility; it was a collaborative effort—not a brute force deployment.

Fast forward to Southern California, to a big, big market. We did the DNPS, the inclusive training, the confirmations of learning, and the negotiation of hitting the dates. What we did wrong was being too impressed with ourselves as the project team and becoming a little too formulaic in our approaches. We thought we were really listening, but there was a subgroup within the greater group that felt left out—the dispatchers. They were left feeling they weren't important enough to the ecosystem in the new world, that their jobs had been marginalized and automated, and that we didn't pay close enough attention to them. With the advent of the new system, phones over clipboards, suddenly there were a whole bunch of things that they used to do that they no longer had to do. The technician could call up the work order himself; he didn't have to talk to somebody back in the call center to authorize the services on an account. Technicians could make edits to the account, they could sell services, and they could do it all from their phone. Dispatchers decided that they were going to torpedo the whole thing because they believed their jobs were being eliminated.

What we didn't do as a project team in that case was make the "why" clear enough to them—why it was going to not only make their jobs easier but was also going to make them more important, because they would be doing more advanced things other than just talking on the phone and pushing buttons.

When it came down to deployment day, we had some monkey wrenches thrown into the deployment for the first three weeks. We had to stop everything and explain to the dispatchers that they needed to support the change. Until the cutover was complete, they had to do their former jobs using old processes. In that case, we hadn't been inclusive enough talking about the future state with one of the processes within the greater change effort. Lesson learned: "inclusive" means inclusive of everybody, not *almost* everybody.

In any case, it doesn't matter how small or large the group. You have to be sensitive to their "why": Why change? Why is it important to me? Why does it make my life easier? In some cases it doesn't, but you have to address it up front, because they're going to figure it out. You might as well sit them down and say, "Yes, you're screwed," so they can decide whether they want to stay or not. You're not going to trick them. This has to do with the whole concept of inclusion. If you can't trust your employees, then you have bigger issues. You need to give them the information. You need to trust that they want to do a good job. If you don't know the "why" and can't share it with them, then they're not going to want to change. They feel like they're doing a pretty darn good job as they sit. Empowering them with analytics and information helps everyone navigate the change and the effect that it has on their "why."

We've also seen backsliding, even in successful change efforts or initiatives within big companies. Even when it's successful, sometimes our clients go awry because the "C's" go back into context mode. You must guard against dropping the rigor when you start celebrating the achievement of the change project. You have done a good job, and you have been inclusive and sympathetic. Then change gets implemented, and you talk about it in contextual terms when you are doing your measurement, but it is not going to stick, because your front line isn't seeing the validation of their "why," even though you may very well have done it. It is up to middle management to make sure that the interface that gets set up at the DNPS continues forever within the company. That is where the sharing of information and the trust is manifested.

And it is not just the front line that pushes back against change: there is plenty of pushback no matter where you are in the organization. At the frontline level, there is pushback to context without content. At the C-level, there is pushback to content without context. They are different languages.

That's why I feel it is more fruitful to engage an interpreter who isn't encumbered by the stigma of politics. It is not incumbent on the frontline employees (FLEs) to be the only ones who change. Part of asking your frontline employees to change involves some change at the C-level; typically, this change includes the mind-set about the sharing of information and a commitment to creating a culture of "open book management." There is plenty of change to go around. It is really about a relationship of respect for the roles that each of those successive levels plays in the ultimate mission, even though the connectivity to that mission is different based on your level. You have to humanize the C-level as well as the FLE level.

"Cs" are afraid that their value is lessened if they are forthcoming with all the information. They still believe in the industrial revolutionary cliché that knowledge is power. I think the progressive organizations are better at it, but they are not perfect. This is not a process in which you can "set it and forget it." It requires a change in adaptability. There will always be people who are playing politics. It is my belief that if you run the organization with integrity and ethics that you size and design for those that want to work within that system, then the bad apples will surface. All that's needed is a mechanism for getting rid of them.

Not everybody is going to fit into this new world order that this book is suggesting. If you cannot change people, you can still ask them to change their behavior and give them structures under which they can accomplish that task. You are not going to get all the people to change, so sometimes you have to "change out" the people. Make sure that your hiring criteria emphasize customer empathy and a commitment to serve. That may change how you employ and whom you employ.

Coming up with a profile that best represents what your ideal employee attitudes should be, is the first thing. Then you evaluate the current staff. Next, honestly communicate about those you suspect will have problems with the new world order and give them an opportunity to fit within it. If they cannot fit in, then you need to manage them out. As critical as it is to figure out whom you want to hire, it is more important to figure out the behaviors that you will not tolerate. Much of success is about the things you choose not to do, as opposed to the things that you do.

The best place to start is determining who *not* to hire. "Who do we want?" is currently the way everybody approaches recruiting and interviewing. "We're looking for this, this, this, and this." They are looking at company values or mission statements, which all read about the same. What are we not going to do? Southwest Airlines is very clear on this; in effect, their message is, either you have a sense of humor, or fly with someone else.

Getting clear on what you will not tolerate is a good thing, but getting clear on what you are not looking for is better. It sounds like a simple reverse, but it is a lot harder to sit down and figure out the behaviors that would make you pass on hiring. Because you are focused on finding certain abilities, you ignore these other qualities:

Annoying habits that they have or choices that they make or personality quirks that they have. After hiring you say, "Whoa, this isn't the guy who came to the interview." Employers want to believe, "They lied during their interview. They put on a show." That might be true, but you cannot control lying. That is just a really convenient excuse because you can control the questions.

You are hiring. *You* are in control. *Ask the questions.* What are you looking to exclude? You will find better people if you interview in that way. To put this in as a system and perpetuate the culture of change, you must hire the right people, but you must first define what that is.

Start with, "Have you served customers before? Tell me about a time when this...? What happened when that...? What did you do here?" Find out how committed to the customer they are. How committed are you? This is not "think customer first," and it is not "do anything that the customer requests," but it does require putting yourself in the customer's mind-set: How would the work I'm doing today in my silo affect the customer?

Most companies still cannot hire with the proper mind-set. It seems that would be pretty low-hanging fruit. If it is so simple, then why do we have all these companies (banks, cable, airlines, etc.) whose customers hate them? How many bad help desk experiences have you had with online shopping on Cyber Monday and Black Friday? I have had a few. Amazon is pretty good at customer service, but they delivered a 50-inch TV to me with a crack in it. They did everything but say, "You're lying. You broke it." How does the guy in shipping affect the customer? Do you believe he thinks about that? In good companies, he does.

All this is important, so pay attention to it: *You have to connect the "why" of each and every person in your organization to the customer. Why are you here?* Amgen was famous for a reporter asking one of their janitors what he did for a living. He answered, "I save lives." He is a janitor at a drug company, but he sees himself as part of a team that makes drugs that save lives. Amgen has done a really good job of connecting that janitor to the doctors and researchers. This is not calculus here. It is pretty simple. As a middle manager you may ask, "How do we affect the customer?" Sometimes you may affect a customer by the way you interact with your peers in the next silo. Spend five minutes a day thinking about it, and I guarantee your operations will get better. Spend five minutes a day with your team thinking about how each of you affects the customer and what you are going to do to improve that interaction. Empower the frontline employees by giving them the authority and responsibility for resolution of problems.

What are you going to do? One thing you can do is slow down. Why are we making so many mistakes? Well, we are going too fast, so we are serving a lot of people poorly. I would suspect that an accountant in your organization could figure this out for you: serving a lot of people badly is probably not as profitable as serving fewer people well. Why? Because the cost of acquisition of a new customer is so many times greater than what it costs to keep an existing customer. Aligning those goals across the departments and divisions is really about each individual's "why," each individual group's "why," and each individual part of the process's "why."

The first step is deciding how to make the customer happier. Once you get those creative juices going, and you have identified how you connect to the customer, then, and only then, can you figure out how to delight the customer as it relates to your content. You want to delight the customer, which may be a complete surprise to the customer—depending on where they are sitting above or below the line of ambivalence. Okay. How can you do better? How can you delight them? Especially if you're in one of the big-five most-hated businesses, you are not going to move quickly from, "My customer hates me and would like nothing better than to watch me die," to "my customer is delighted." It is going to take time and creative effort. You have to shock the heck out of them, probably several times, with some kind of demonstration of caring. The first time you do it, they are going to think that they just happened to get the one good person who works at the company. That may have to happen six or seven times to get them to believe, "Wow, this is really changing."

Just keep moving forward. You will get there.

CHAPTER 8

BOILING THE OCEAN

How to prioritize the change process.

I learned that we can do anything, but we can't do everything ...
at least not at the same time. So think of your priorities
not in terms of what activities you do, but when
you do them. Timing is everything.
—Dan Millman

I believe with all my heart in the Cube of Opportunity. I believe the Cube of Opportunity allows decision makers to put a defensible structure around the decision-making process when socializing it both up and down their command chain. It allows a decision maker to separate the wheat from the chaff and make a decision that has some precision and planning.

The original idea behind the Cube of Opportunity was to inject a measurable third construct to decision making and put it in a graphical format that provides leverage in a presentation.

The Cube of Opportunity:

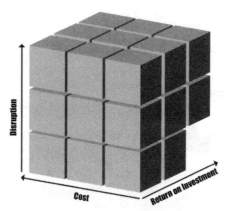

Low Disruption, Low Cost, High Return on Investment

Figure 12

We have reduced everything about a project proposal to three measures with the Cube of Opportunity—cost, disruption, and return on investment (ROI). Two of the measures are inverse, where a score of "one" is good and a score of "three" is bad. The two inverse measures are "disruption" and "cost"—where more is not good! Then a bad investment is one that is high cost, high disruption, and low return on investment (ROI). It is important to understand that the aggregate score of a particular project is not necessarily the determinate of a go vs. a no-go decision, meaning "better" isn't the bigger number. The cube of opportunity is a structure that allows decision makers to score the relative value of various projects against one another and sequence them in a way that increases their organizational change maturity. A "one" with respect to disruption would equate to a low level of disruption. A "three" would be high disruption. Obviously, one is more desirable than three in this case.

The same applies to cost: a score of one would be low, and a three would be high cost. With respect to the return on investment (ROI) construct, a one is bad and a three is good. So what you are ideally looking for is "one, one, three"; that is the sweet spot (see fig. 12). Line all your projects up and place them like a child's blocks, with each individual block representing a project. Then, put them in a three by three cube, similar to a Rubik's Cube, if you view it from the side. Where does each block representing each project fit? If it is in the top corner, then you're in good shape. If it is not there or you don't have anything there, then you go to the next level: What's more important, a higher ROI or lower disruption?

As the person asserting this concept, I would say at the beginning of introducing change as the "way of the future," you want to start with a project that has a low level of disruption. If you don't have a project that is minimally disruptive, then you need to find one that is, or add additional resources to the project in an effort to make the project as minimally disruptive as you can, which will probably increase the cost and thus move it around in relation to other projects being considered.

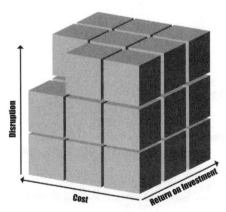

High Disruption, High Cost, Low Return on Investment

Figure 13

In decision-making meetings, it is popular to weigh risk against reward. Those are two common constructs and usually boil down to cost versus expected ROI. Depending on how you spin it, it really comes down to, "What are we going to get, and what's it going to cost us?" What we found out is that those two constructs don't help very much when estimating the *success probability* of a change effort: the adoption rate of the necessary change by those who need to commit will be the driving factor in whether the effort succeeds or fails. That, we have found, has more to do with disruption, a more politically correct label for the reactions that I identified as toxic naysayers earlier in this book. Disruption is specifically related to how much change the people within the system must accept. By ranking that third construct against the tried-and-true constructs of ROI and investment, you get a more robust, thoughtful evaluation of the things that you will need to do and the implementation timeline required to make the change stick. When you sit down and look more closely at who is going to be disruptive or disrupted, it calls into question things that don't typically get discussed when a change effort is being evaluated on cost vs ROI.

Part of the reason that disruption doesn't get discussed is because management wants to believe that change will happen based on brute force deployment, via the dispensation of initiative or a memo—and it is not unreasonable to *think* that. But it is unreasonable to *believe* that, given 100 years of modern business history. I am not aware of a single case study reflecting a brute force deployment as a *model* of efficiency and *long-term* success—but there are plenty of failures. Anybody reading this book can likely identify a failed project in which they were involved that employed the brute force tactic.

The Cube of Opportunity is a tool that forces the project team and the management team to think through the third construct of disruption. It shouldn't come as a surprise that what we typically find is that it is best to implement a project that minimizes the associated disruption and expenses while maximizing the return on investment.

What you want to settle on as a starting place is a project that causes the minimum number of people to "tilt," does not require a great big investment, and produces some visible results that can be celebrated. The objective of a multi-phased change effort is to create a culture which change is expected, accepted, and embraced. To be successful, the creation of a change culture will require several small change efforts before embarking on a larger change-oriented project. Typically, when you work in big companies, there are hundreds of things to work on, and it is human nature to go after the biggest problem, thinking, "Well, if we could just fix this one thing, then all the other things will fall into place." I don't disagree with that theory, but I do disagree with the methodology. I believe that fixing one thing, two things, or three things begins an ongoing momentum of change that will drive a company forward.

Let's say you are looking at 10 or 12 things requiring some level of change, as identified by the operational team, audit team, or whoever has been appointed to look at operations. They have determined that some kind of adjustment to people, process, or tools is necessary. To be successful, this is the point where you need to sit down and talk through the Cube of Opportunity and the three constructs to determine "Which one will get adopted the fastest based on the fact that it is the least disruptive?" At AT&T Broadband, the company was launching telephony over cable, and hundreds of things went wrong because they did not complete the critical upfront planning. The tendency was to isolate the efforts on whatever piece of the process was the most problematic: what was causing the most jobs, or the most installations, to fail. What it came down to was that the

CRM workflow manager, also known as the billing system in cable, was the biggest problem. While this was true, it was also going to take the longest and be the most invasive and expensive problem to fix. It had one attractive feature to it: it didn't require internal change! Everything could be *blamed* on the vendor.

Many times, companies look at root cause analysis and come up with six or seven issues, and the one that is ultimately the focus is the one that requires change by an outside vendor. This avoids internal change, which satisfies the human condition of not wanting to change, and in this case it also satisfied the condition of, "This is really the biggest problem." The problem at AT&T Broadband was that it was not going to result in any kind of ROI, either over the short term or the long term. And it was going to take more than a year to effect the change.

With the lack of attention to the third construct in the Cube of Opportunity concept, AT&T Broadband went ahead with trying to force the billing system vendor to change the way the system worked, in parallel with its continued efforts to deploy the new product. The result was a horrible disaster and ultimately required restarting the entire project. There were many casualties along the way, and that experience is what created our mantra of "Slow down to go fast." The entire thought process behind the Cube of Opportunity is linked to this concept. Many times, big enterprises want to go fast. Moving fast can result in hasty decisions, and under the cover of the hasty decision, there is usually something related to a lack of willingness to change. That lack of willingness might be for either political reasons or wanting the ability

> The way you get people to change is to involve them in the process, because people will adopt what they help create.

to push it off onto some other entity, like an outside vendor. The problem is that the internal people using a particular process or tool also must change, and there is typically no effort put into changing the internal resources methods and procedures.

When evaluating a project, management will use the X- and Y-axes of a chart reflecting (1) return on investment and (2) the cost of the project. Those are pretty straightforward. The third axis, the Z-axis which creates the three-dimensional graph (or cube in this case), is disruption. Another reason that the Z-axis isn't a primary focus is because it is fairly subjective, as there is no way to quantifiably measure anticipated disruption (see fig. 13 pg. 99). To put a measure on disruption, you must understand your organization. You must be sympathetic to those who are going to change. What you cannot do is say, "I don't care how disruptive it is because I'm just going to write a memo, and they will do what I tell them to do." If that is your attitude, then you are always going to register zero disruption, because you are not really being authentic about what you are asking the people within the system to do. Accept the idea that people aren't going to want to change just because it is your brilliant idea.

The third axis, disruption, is really where the magic of change happens. I believe it is a short step toward the overall notion that change is about adoption, not about the actual project. The question is, "How do you get people to change?" and the way you get people to change is to involve them in the process, because people will adopt what they help create. That is what the disruption construct of the Cube of Opportunity is there to assess. You look at a project and you say, "Okay, these change projects are going to cost X dollars. We expect X+Y dollars in return. That's pretty darn good."

The next question is, "What and who needs to change?"

"Well, there are tens of thousands of employees that need to change the way that they do their jobs."

"Hmm, that's no small thing. What's that really going to cost? What's the downtime going to be? What's the training time going to be? How long will the timeline to get buy-in be? How many dog and pony shows are we going to need to do?"

In short, "How complicated is it going to be to get adoption?"

WHO ARE YOUR CHANGE AGENTS?

Can you spot your change agents? The most obvious ones are those who have nothing to lose and everything to gain or those who can risk it all and still lose nothing. These are typically people who are on their way out or new hires who want to make a difference. The new hires want their project to be successful, so they may be a little bit easier to convince to be supportive of the change effort, as compared to the people within the existing system who need to change.

Have you heard the story of the new executive and the three envelopes?

> John, a brand new, starry-eyed executive is excited about his new position at the C-level when he arrives on his first day. He is about two hours early because he is so amped up, and he goes skipping into his new corner office. He is surprised to see that the guy he is replacing is still there packing his stuff. The outgoing executive says, "Come in, John. I've just got a few more things to pack up. I'll be out of here in a minute. We didn't expect you until eight."

John says, "Well, Jerry, I'm so excited. I just wanted to get here early and get things set up."

Jerry says, "I understand. Just give me a few more minutes." Jerry is packing up his stuff and John just sits there, feeling uncomfortable.

Mostly to make conversation, he says, "So what words of advice might you have for me, Jerry, as the outgoing old dog?"

Jerry tells him, "I'm going to leave these three envelopes in the top drawer, and they're numbered one, two, and three. So when things start getting bad, just open up number one and there's a slip of paper inside, and so on and so forth, as your career unfolds." He finishes packing his pictures and walks out.

John says to himself, "That crazy old man. No wonder they got rid of him." So John sits at his new desk, and for about three to four weeks things are okay, because he is the new guy. After about six weeks, things start getting a little tougher; he is digging around in his desk one morning and sees these three envelopes. Naturally, he gets curious. He pulls out envelope number one and opens it up. There's a slip of paper inside that says, "Blame everything on your predecessor." John thinks about it for a moment and he goes, "Well, you know what? That is true. I'm just trying to clean his mess. It's going to take me a while."

That works for six to eight months, and John keeps diligently working away while the heat is off until a new project fails. He is there late at night and again happens to be looking for something in the center drawer of his desk. He pulls out envelope number two, and he opens it up, and the slip of paper inside says, "Reorganize." John says, "I was thinking about doing that. I need to make some changes happen here." So he goes in and starts reorganizing staff and roles, and that works for about a year.

Then comes that day he sees envelope number three, and he pulls it out and he opens it, and inside the piece of paper says, "Prepare three envelopes."

This is the way business is run because the only way to change is to get rid of people and bring in somebody who has the courage to make change—but not until they have blamed everything on their predecessor. Businesses would be better off if we weren't all just waiting to prepare three envelopes.

Better doesn't come without some failure. You don't learn about business from successes, you learn about business from failures. You learn about *yourself* from successes.

So who are your ideal change agents? Truly, they are those who have courage. How their courage manifests itself depends on the situation. The objective of this book is to encourage people to step up and have the courage to be first. You employ the Cube of Opportunity, and you try to stack the odds in your favor. Business and the media tend to hang leaders when they are wrong. But in reality, the most important goal should be to create a culture where getting better is the objective every day, as opposed to attempting to be right all the time.

When I think about successful change agents I have encountered, the size of the success usually isn't as impactful as the shock of who pulled it off. You always hear about these rags-to-riches, overnight success tales. We love those stories. I worked with a senior vice president in Florida, someone that nobody really knew, who was facing a collision of three different cultures. He was an unassuming guy who believed in change and believed that things needed to move forward. He basically came from nowhere and was sitting next to me at the dog and pony show. I didn't even realize he was a senior vice president, because he was sitting there in a Hawaiian shirt and khakis.

But he happened to be one of the smartest, most effective people I think I have ever worked with. What he pulled off was nothing short of Herculean. It really had to do with him understanding that the employees under his command needed to change, being resolute in giving them the time and tools to make the change, and trusting in the people who reported to him to guide that change. They went from being the worst in the market to the absolute best in a span of about eight months, despite tremendous obstacles.

What made him so effective? He had clarity of mission and an understanding of what a change to standard operating procedures would entail. He was able to communicate not only his resolve but also his commitment to helping everybody adjust. He understood the relationship between "important" vs. "urgent" (see fig. 14). Don't confuse the "urgent" with the "important" often they are vastly different.

Figure 14

Certainly, it is not always an executive who is an effective agent. There was a technical supervisor who had some ideas of process and procedure changes that would gain efficiencies and leverage output, and it did not require people working harder or longer. It was truly a "working smarter" idea; he believed that changing the blade in your cable cutter every Monday, no matter how many times you had used it the week before, would be a way to increase productivity. His hypothesis was that when the blade gets dull, it takes longer to get it to cut through cable. If you have a sharp blade, you can do it with one cut, and the fractions of a second that were saved every time you avoid using a dull blade would add up. He pushed his idea that they should change that blade more often, rather than whenever they felt like it. He met with some objection, because suddenly they were going through twice as many blades as they had over the same time period in the past. But he was able to point to the fact that they were getting more work done, and that recovered the cost. It was a small, simple change, but it produced a meaningful result.

Creating organizational clarity starts with an internal investigation on your strategy and your operational construct. Where are you going and why? Next comes evaluating the resources—people, processes, and tools—needed to get there and, looking at each of those components, asking, "Are these adequate? Are they best in class? Are they over-engineered? Are they under-engineered?" Then you must create messaging directed at the internal human resources: the people, the processes they follow, and the tools they use. With respect to the tools, you have to communicate to the vendors who provide them.

Organizational clarity also requires understanding your mission and vision, and the connectivity between your operational capabilities to your mission and vision. Next, communicate that down to the tactical level, so that everybody understands how those things connect. That is the job of leadership—in fact, the sole job of leadership. Just like *Undercover Boss* shows us every week, you get that organizational clarity by descending from the Ivory Tower of C-Suite, getting out on the front lines, and actually seeing what your employees are doing to execute on the vision—or at least their interpretation of the vision. Everybody from the very top to the front lines—from Cs to FLEs—understands what the organization is there to do; they understand their place in the organization, and that is how the product or service flows out to the customer.

Many executives rely on marketing to fulfill this requirement. They know messaging and marketing tell the customers what the companies are doing for them. But who is speaking to the employees? Presumably, employees see the advertising, but there is disconnection between what you are telling your customer and the way you are acting internally, which doesn't create organizational clarity. It creates organizational chaos, conflict, and hypocritical messaging. If you are counting on your frontline resources understanding their mission because of the slogans that you are pumping out to your customers, you are probably selling yourself short.

DEVELOPING SYSTEMS AROUND ORGANIZATIONAL CLARITY

The systems that you have in place to support your mission, your vision, and your organization have certain values and beliefs within them. One of them probably has to do with the fair and honest treatment of employees and customers. The system that you have in place to compensate and incentivize your employee should be consistent with that value. So how do your human systems—vacation requests, sick time, etc.—work? How does your payroll work? How does your time tracking work? Are they consistent with an open architecture where people are trusted, or do you say, "Yes, we trust our employees, but they have to badge in and out of the building because we don't really trust them to be here"?

If your systems are at odds with your messaging, you are going to be seen as hypocritical, and that is going to come through in your frontline employees' interactions with their customers. It manifests itself on the phone; for instance, when an agent for a company on the phone with a customer say things like, "Yeah, I don't know why I have to do this either. I hate to do this to you, but I have to do it this way because it's the way the system makes me do this," or, "I care about your satisfaction as a customer. However I'm going to make you enter your information six times before you get to talk to somebody who can help you." Clearly, that agent doesn't care about the customer's time. "We're here to help. Did you know you can also go on the web and help yourself?" Those aren't systems that are consistent with the messaging. When you're inconsistent with the messaging, you might as well not be messaging at all because what you say isn't what you do.

"We know your time is valuable. Your wait will be 17 minutes." Clearly you don't know the true value of my time. Those are just words, and as the Chinese proverb says, words don't cook rice, only water and heat cook rice.

Everybody who has an IVR system could institute a change like this: "Our wait time is longer than we want to ask you to hold on the phone. If you would prefer, punch in the number where we can call you back in 12 minutes; or if you wish, you can remain on hold." Put the control back in the customer's hands. "We know your time is valuable." A psychologist or organizational management consultant told you that you *should* say that—but you are not acting that way. Why aren't you acting that way? *Because your systems are not created to allow your human resources to honor your mission.*

Where to start? Start somewhere. Every process is a system. Every computer application is a system. How do you eat the elephant? One bite at a time.

Start with your employee manual; how is time entry handled, or scheduling, or time off requests? How are incoming calls are handled? How does triage work when a customer calls in? How does the call get routed?

Somebody is deciding this stuff—although many times the people making the decisions are the providers of the software solutions, outside the company, and they do not care about your company like you do. It is not that vendors don't care, they just don't care like you do. They don't care like your employees do. No one cares about your business like you do. Why? *Because it is not their business.* Software vendors care about their business, which is selling you more software and increasing their margins. They don't make more money by spending more time with you and helping you make these decisions, so you are going to have to demand that they do that, or you are going to have to do it. Because somebody is going to have to do it, and I would suggest that that somebody come from inside the company. Do you also hire somebody from outside that company? Yes—to help you focus on these things and to help you identify issues and make decisions. Did anybody sit down and really go through the IVR triage process and say, "Okay. You can say this, this, or this. Here's what's in the customer's head if you say this, and here's what's in their head if you do this. Here's where it's going to cost you more money. But on the other end, your customer is going to be happy."

> It is not that vendors don't care, they just don't care like you do.

Those are all system decisions; how do the decisions usually get made? By following industry best practices: "This software package has all these features, and they do it for three of our competitors, and they seem to be doing well." The phrase "industry best practice" is the bane of change. We all know the industry best practice. The problem is, you can't stop there if you want to be a leader in the industry.

You have to say, "So this is how my industry does it—but maybe this is an opportunity for us to do it better and different. Let's make a change to this industry best practice and we'll be best in class."

Everyone wants to talk like they are best in class—but few want to actually do the work to be best in class. There are so many other things to worry about.

OVER-COMMUNICATE ORGANIZATIONAL CLARITY

We have all heard the pop psychology/marketing data that indicates that the amount of images and input that we get daily is so overwhelming that in order to stand out in a crowd, people need to hear, understand, and consider the same message seven or eight times. That means you may need to show it to them 100 times, because they're going to be thinking about something else or texting while you are talking to them. Have you ever been in a room where there are 20 people participating on the same webinar, but there is only one person who is actually listening to the presenter? That is the person who set up the webinar.

I meet with my staff every Friday morning at 9:30, and I do a ten-minute talk. This is where I try to live what I'm preaching, where I over-communicate organizational clarity and review the goals, the mission, the vision, and our "why." I have to do it over and over and over to the point where I can do it in my sleep. As leaders, we don't like to repeat ourselves because we get bored with our own messages. But the truth is that until you are bored with it, you haven't said it enough. Until you think it is going to make you sick to parrot your mission one more time, along with your vision, your systems, and the organizational clarity—you haven't done it enough.

Until you hear your words coming out of your staff's mouth, they don't have it. They have a version of it, but it might not be your version of it, so you have to over-communicate it, especially because you will probably end up changing it a bit year-over-year. We forecast, we change directions, and we change strategy, so it is a constant process of over-communication because people will say, "Oh, we've changed strategy, so this part of it is gone."

"Well, no. We didn't change that part of it. We didn't say that."

"Well, I just thought it was assumed that the only things that changed were the things that I changed."

"No, we want to change the part of the strategy we didn't like." We hire people for their brains, and damned if they don't always want to use them. So if you want them to use them in a way that is congruent with your plan, then you need to be telling them the plan all the time. You empower people with data every day, even twice a day if possible—early and often. Empower with data and over-communicate the elements of organizational clarity, from top to bottom.

The idea is that everybody has equal and open access to numbers and to information. So what do you want them to know? Tell them. Management tends to think based on history and that anytime anybody wants to know something it is because they are upset or they are trying to catch you doing something wrong. The truth of the matter is if you are doing something wrong, then you deserve to be caught.

Here is a little tip: do not do anything wrong and the information won't hurt you. If you are not hiding anything, then why do you care if your employees see it? "Well, they might get the wrong idea." Well, if they get the wrong idea, then you're not communicating organizational clarity. You're not escaping this, Mr. Manager or Ms. Leader: Information cannot be used against you if it's righteous and if you're clear about your mission, your goal, your vision, and the "why." It should not be an "us versus them" type of work environment. Over-communicate, and you just might get through.

FIND WAYS TO FACILITATE COMMUNICATION BETWEEN SILOS

Right now the cable business is undergoing extreme reshuffling, and the fear of change is everywhere. You can imagine the turmoil inside the industry, especially among the people inside the different silos within these companies, who are wondering whether they will be the survivors or the incumbents, or whether they are somewhere in the middle and will be traded. Do they retire, do they get a new job, or do they stay while the transition is going on? The transition is going to probably take two years, if not longer. There isn't anything new here—business is always changing.

Chaos is very fertile ground for outside consultants to come in and try to at least get everybody back in the boat: some people have a very firm grasp on the sides, and they are just trying not to get thrown out of the boat, while others are standing up, creating all the turmoil, and trying to knock those other people out. There are decisions being made that are not based on any kind of continuity of business. Things need to change, but since we don't have a culture that facilitates change and we don't have good communications between the silos, the decisions that are being made are based solely on emotion and expedience and really don't have a lot to do with good thought and planning. Thus, they are losing good people that they probably should keep strategically. They are keeping people who are not necessarily the best.

It comes down to not having a good plan for understanding the organization silo to silo, side to side, top to bottom, and Cs to FLEs because so many things need to change all at once that the decisions are haphazard and are made with precious little input or consideration as to what the real future holds. How do we change that? How

115

do we prepare ourselves for change? I think the best way to do that is to facilitate the conversations between silos ahead of time.

I was talking with one of my sales guys about what is going to happen to some of the people that we have been marketing to or doing business with for years, that we would consider our champions. Are they going to ride off into the sunset? A lot of executives are taking packages and running, people that the companies didn't necessarily want to lose. They don't see how or where they have a role in the new "why," so they're outta there. I'm talking mostly about executives who are getting seven-figure windfall packages who have been managing a silo. They believe that they understand business, and they believe they understand what intention to retention really means. I saw this in 1999–2000 when AT&T bought Telecommunications Inc. (TCI). I saw it again in 2002 and 2003, when Comcast bought AT&T Broadband. Then I saw it at Sun Microsystems when they did a huge reorganization in 2004–2005—executives getting big packages and going out into the workforce or deciding to start their own businesses. Sometimes they take a job at a smaller company with more expansive responsibility, the theory being if you have a senior VP who managed a large silo in a multi-billion dollar company with 20,000 people, then that person could probably be CEO of a 1,000-person company. The problem is that even though it was a really big silo, that is all it was—a really big silo. What I saw were these same people failing because they didn't understand the concept of intention to retention, which is, in short, the communication *between* silos.

When you have good communication from intention to retention (silo to silo), you understand the "why," which is analogous to what we now call the "customer journey." When that hasn't been your experience and is suddenly required of you, it's different. I would estimate that 99 percent of these executives-turned-entrepreneur went out of business within the first two years, in each of those three eras, and in two different industries with hundreds of people. This was primarily because they didn't understand the necessity of every silo in the system.

Management's responsibility is to traffic information up and down and to facilitate the buy-in between the silos. How do you do that? Again, communication starts with understanding what your message is. The more transparent you can be with your front line, then the more honest you can be, and the messaging is easier. No worries about being afraid to share information that causes a problem because eventually the truth will come out. Of course, if I ask you, you will say you want to be transparent, you want to be honest, open, and ethical—all of those great values that everybody talks about. They all look great in a mission/vision statement, but ask yourself, "What does that mean to me in the context of running my business and sharing information with my people? What's my message going to be?" Is it consistent with the values that you have in your organization? Too often that stuff gets shoved into a drawer and doesn't get applied when you get down to the operation level—the tactical level—because this is tough stuff. The "need to know" filter gets snapped on: "Do they need to know that?" The short answer is, yes. If you want innovation and if you want transparency, "they" need to know everything.

So—first know what your message is, then look at how you are going to communicate it. Most executives default to, "I will write a memo." As executives, what we're thinking is, "What's the easiest way for me to get to the most people?" But you need to have more arrows in your quiver and use more modalities of communication to reach your audience because you are marketing ideas here, just like someone marketing a book or a seminar. What is the best way to communicate between silos?

It might not be an email (and I know that is scary because that means you will have to go and talk to somebody). It might not be a PowerPoint demonstration. It might not be a webinar that will stream live at 10 a.m. on the third Thursday of the month … and then again, it might be. But here is the thing—we know that there are generally three different ways in which people learn: aural, visual, and kinesthetic. That would suggest that if you are addressing a group of more than three, you are going to have to parse your message in each of the three different modalities if you really want to reach them because the odds are good that email just is not going to work for 80 percent, much less 100 percent, of your intended target. Or are you going to say, "That's the way it is, they will adjust to me"? That worked in the Industrial Revolution because people needed a job, but people today don't buy into that. How do you communicate to a group in a large organization? What do you want to communicate? Why are you willing to communicate it? How will you go about communicating it?

You have to be willing to over-communicate, using all modalities, until you are hearing your own words coming back at you, because when the messages come back you know they are becoming part of your culture. You have to get your leadership to buy into this strategy so that they start talking about how they are going to communicate with one another. If they are communicating with one another, the content of it will come together. I believe that the time spent on this up front is time you gain on the backend; slow down to go fast. Once you have the conduit open, the communication can flow more freely, more efficiently, and more simply because it is a relationship built on trust, transparency, and a shared goal.

How do you do it? As in jiu jitsu, you use what you have; there is a great diversity of styles, beliefs, orientations, and value sets. Embrace the diversity, the lack of sameness, and use it to your advantage. We need to communicate more and differently. That very crisp memo may be good between executives, because they all have the same kind of orientation. As you look at profiles of type-A personalities, who typically are the ones who rise to the top of the organization, they all communicate fairly well with one another because they usually have the same communication style. These are people who have, somehow in their journey up the ladder, forgotten about salutations and closings on emails. Those are not necessary. They forget about capitalization and punctuation and actual sentence structure. They insist in their own defense that it is more efficient, but it does not build trust and transparency. Without follow up, it doesn't quantify, qualify, or verify the recipient's understanding.

Commit to going from being reactive to being proactive, then to being preemptive. It is a process, but change is a process. It requires commitment to creating a culture of transparency, change and communication, because that is what is ultimately going to drive everything. The goal is to get everyone to start talking about the "why" of change; the momentum of moving along the continuum is how you harness the winds of change.

What will the conversation be about? "Why this is good" is certainly where everybody likes to start, but the "why it's good" is probably the most dangerous place to start because that is not the kneejerk reaction by most humans. Most humans only want to know how they are getting screwed by the change. My tactic on this, without letting it becoming a complaint session, is to openly talk about why it is *bad*, with the caveat that you have to agree that you are going to give equal time to the good. Then, in the middle, you have those things that we call the issues and risks. Why is the change good? Why is the change bad? "Bad" means, what are we afraid of? Really, most of the time, it comes down to risks.

The first reaction is to search for reasons not to proceed, which is reflective of human conditioning. The majority of us don't like or want change, so let's find a reason to kill it. Many people reflexively push back, perhaps because they are "Debbie Downer" or because they don't have enough information, or they simply need time to reflect. If we make assumptions about why the proposed change is bad, then we can avoid the change and move on to do something more interesting. A closer look at the assumptions we utilize to stop change typically reveals the risks involved. Identifying and getting the perceived risks out on the table is a good way to start. We will not solve each issue as it is discussed, but we get the organization talking about change, the possibilities of change, and we begin to formulate mitigation plans for the risks. This is where the buy-in and creation of the change effort happens. This is where people start adopting because they are helping to create the change plan. This can only happen if there is trust that allows communication that, in its best form, will contain some amount of conflict.

This is what classic sales training was all about: changing a person's mind and forcibly tricking them into something. This is the reason why people don't like to be sold to. It is why in response to, "Can I help you today?" they like to say, "NO!"

"No, I'm just looking"—yet clearly, they are here with a purpose. Nobody feels comfortable saying, "Yes, I came here looking for a little black dress."

This is because we are afraid of hearing, "We don't have a black dress so let me just cram you in a little green dress." Why? Because the salesperson has not earned our trust.

The new style of sales training is about learning how companies and individuals buy—not forcibly changing their buying criteria but helping them to understand value. It requires that you as the seller understand what they want. That discovery process is mutual; the customer or the employee also discovers what he or she wants because many times they've started out with only a vague notion. It works the same way when you sell your ideas about change. We address the objections, not by countering or downplaying them but by dealing with them openly so that people can make up their own minds. Open and honest communication will yield better results than forcibly putting down objections that will reappear at a later time when they are more toxic and result in more disruption to the process.

That is the idea about harnessing the winds of change. You must know which ways the winds are blowing and how to adjust your sails. Sailing is a nice analogy here because you don't always get to go as the wind blows to reach the result that you are navigating toward; sometimes you have to tack left and right to navigate the available energy to get where you want to go.

This approach can go wrong when the conversation starts getting lost, when it turns into what I call a nonproductive complaining session. The leader needs to understand this is going to happen, and it is not bad unless you allow it to devolve into a giant mudslinging affair. You will often need to frame your reference point and say, "Why don't we take this back to the customer's point of view?" Ultimately that is what we are here to do; we are here to drive the customer from intention to retention, as far above the line of ambivalence as we possibly can. When we get to the end of the line, "retention," and we start over, we want to come back through the process and drive the customer even higher above the line of ambivalence. The goal is an ever-increasing trust relationship with the customer.

This will never be 100 percent achieved. You are always going to make mistakes, and you are always going to fall down; you have to be happy with being better than you were the day before. The main thing is that this process works, across all industries, and on any scale.

We have employed this methodology over the last 15 years, in retail, fast food, cable, telco, financial services, insurance, credit card processing, banking, and healthcare—it works in any environment. What do these disparate enterprises have in common? Think of the three-legged stool; no matter what the industry, it always involves people engaging with processes and using tools. It is really no more complicated than that. The three things that we can affect are long-term sustainable, repeatable, and transferable types of elements. The treatment of those three elements can be scaled to any size, regardless of whether you are a 12-person, 12,000-person, or a 200,000-person firm.

The customer journey is paramount. The customer journey is represented by "a person that buys," regardless of the product or service; even in business to business, a person is ultimately the decision maker. At the end of the day, it is always those same three components— people, process, and tools—and how they interact that define the customer's journey.

CHAPTER 9

PREPARE ... TO BE PROACTIVE

How to move forward and measure the distance you have traveled.

"We are what we repeatedly do.
Excellence, then, is not an act but a habit."
—Aristotle

There are a few roadblocks to steer clear of in the pursuit of providing an exceptional customer journey. As you chart your path of customer satisfaction from intention to retention, the most direct route is the most effective. This direct route involves breaking down and understanding each customer interaction, whether it is person to person, a process through a person, a tool to a person, or any combination of those things. Everyone at the company must understand the relationship your enterprise has with your customer.

Theoretically, leaders have thought about where they want to go and have a lot of reports and data on where the company has been, at least from the standpoint of traditional measures of facts, figures, and data. Part of understanding the current state is looking at what is being measured. There is a real romance with historical data that is probably born out of the financial industry, despite the insistence that "past results are not indicative of future performance." However, that is what business does on just about every measure; most businesses equate success to doing better than the previous year.

In fact, this kind of measurement is nothing more than a stick—which someone will use to poke another. From that point of view, the best result is to do only slightly better than last year because that way you avoid getting yelled at and avoid having new, unrealistic goals set for the next year. Anyone who is planning on staying with the company does not want to blow away last year's numbers because when next year arrives, this year will be last year, and they'll be expected to surpass this year's numbers. This is a pervasive and sophomoric look at business and measuring the value of how people are performing. It is no longer necessary to use such an unsophisticated approach because the ability to crunch numbers with modern algorithms and pivot many more facts can be done with minimal expense.

So how does a person change the current mind-set that predicts next year's numbers based on today's? Multitask sequencing. Sequencing, or routing, is often described as multitasking. I am a good multitasker because I can sequence my work efficiently—but truthfully, I am only really doing one thing at a time. Research has shown that the idea of doing multiple tasks simultaneously is not efficient. Now, if you organize your thoughts and your processes, you can shrink the amount of time between tasks, compressing them so that it might feel like multitasking—but in fact, it is not. Texting while driving is multitasking, and we know how well that works out. Drunk driving used to be the biggest cause of traffic deaths, but now it is texting while driving. We've become too comfortable with the notion of multitasking, which is basically trying to pay attention to too many things at the same time, and that is beyond our physical human capability.

This is where my favorite saying comes back in: "Slow down to go fast." This means prioritize your task work further out than two seconds, and then go execute it. That is what game plans are. A team has a playbook and then decides what they are going to do. When they go out on the field, everybody understands what his or her role is, and they execute the plan. It is a sequencing of the events, it is routing, and it is dispatching; it is not multitasking, and it is not luck—it is just good preparation.

Now, that is not to say that there isn't an exception to this rule, such as some brilliant person who can just show up and wing it. The problem is that we are not all exceptional; only exceptional people are exceptional. You are going to have to invest the time to become exceptional at execution, which means you are going to have the plan memorized. That is what you need to teach your people because there aren't enough truly exceptional people who you can hire to work for you. What you do have are people who are capable of exceptional things, if you teach them how to sequence their activity. Teach them to interact with one another, show them what is important, and show them that change is good and that sometimes feeling lost in the moment is not a bad thing overall. It is a means to an end—the end being excellent execution.

Failure to measure virtually guarantees failure to improve; the exceptional customer journey can only be achieved through scrupulous measurement and management. It is imperative that you establish a baseline of satisfaction, which presents clarity for your people. For instance, a service organization might determine that no customer should have to call with a problem more than twice a year and then offer some kind of incentive if that base line is not exceeded. Notice I do not advocate the use of a stick if they don't meet or beat that baseline; while negative reinforcement can be effective in the short term, it is not a long-term solution. Most independent free thinkers are not going to be eternally happy in a negative reinforcement situation. It is not that you should never use negative reinforcement, but positive reinforcement has more long-term lasting effects and can be built upon because it extends the relationship of trust and transparency.

Catch people doing things right and make positive examples of those who are meeting or beating the expectation because that creates healthy competition among peers, driving them to new personal bests. The whole concept of a personal best is a motivating thing for most people. If you strive daily to be better than you were the day before, you are going to feel great about yourself. If your boss acknowledges that effort, you are going to feel great about your job, and that kind of employee buy-in to the change effort is what promotes progress toward your ultimate goals.

HOW DO YOU KNOW HOW YOU ARE DOING? SURVEYS ARE GREAT, BUT ...

Performance doesn't mean anything if you can't measure it, but all measurement systems aren't equally useful or accurate. Surveys are good if they are used properly, but the science around creating surveys is complex. It has been proven that there must be a lot of rigor (i.e. science) in constructing surveys in order for them to be valid. Without having exceptional scientific methodologies, standards, and controls, surveys appear to be scientific when they are, in fact, just a bunch of collected and confounded data with the appearance of being authentic. In this case, you talk about things such as examiner bias and leading the respondent—basically coloring the responses.

The biggest trap is putting too much emphasis and belief in the data without a proper amount of control and the right application with respect to the margin of error. When you are making surveys, there are many rules and standard statistical requirements that Six Sigma methods can help with in order to get representative sampling and statistical significance around different confidence levels.

The trap is accepting a tiny sampling as a larger truth. For a company with millions of customers to only talk to three customers about what's going to be done for the annual strategy is not a statistically significant sample. Results are meaningless without a statistically significant size and proper sampling design.

A survey also requires some controls around the survey taking itself, such as the way the questions are written, the way the questions are asked, and who is asking them. Is it a one-on-one survey, a pen-and-paper survey, or a web-based survey? Writing good survey questions that will yield useful data is not an exercise for amateurs. You can't just blast out an email survey that your intern put together with SurveyMonkey and call that anything other than a straw poll.

The big fallacy is convincing yourself that, because you have survey results, you have statistically significant information, despite the fact it wasn't scientifically constructed. If you are going to do surveys, then you need to ensure that they are done properly with the correct protocols and adjust for, or at least consider, factors such as examiner bias. You must be aware of the fact that if you are asking a customer a question, whether it is on the phone or in person, you are going to inject some kind of bias into the process because of the interaction. You have injected a variable that changes the playing field. It is worth the investment to hire someone who can prepare a proper survey. If you are going to use it to base your strategy and operational execution, then it is absolutely essential to do what is necessary to ensure that the data you collect isn't confounded from the beginning.

This is also my issue with focus groups or mall surveys. The problem is that when you just walk up to somebody and start asking them questions, it is not the same as putting your product on the shelf against competitor products and having somebody walk down the aisle and make a choice. In a focus group or survey, you are putting that consumer in a position where they have to make a choice in an artificial environment. It is no different than when focus groups were used to test ads at malls—surveyors would grab people off the concourse and have them sit down in a room to watch a commercial. That is about as artificial an environment as you can get.

When you put a commercial on the air, the chances are good that many viewers will simply fast-forward past it. Today, nobody can be forced to watch an ad. So that kind of sampling and survey has its limitations, and the pitfall is the danger that you will believe your own hype. You must adjust for those contingencies.

That leads to indirect routing: An executive says, "Get me a survey about what the take rate (i.e., close rate) would be on this particular product." The marketing department gets together, and they mock up an ad. Even better, if it is a big company, the marketing department puts together simple requirements, and they go out to three agencies, and those agencies come up with ads, and then they pick the one they like the best. There is already a problem because the consumers haven't been consulted. So what you are actually getting is a set of requirements that amount to an idea, which then gets broken into three different ideas. One of those ideas then goes to what is now the second-removed outsourced company, who takes it and turns it into a survey. Then it is handed off to a bunch of employees, who go out and execute on the survey with either customers or the public at large. Dilution complete.

That is a simplified example of an indirect route. Generally, there are more steps involved. The results get compiled and sometimes massaged around as the reports get rolled up. The research is the conglomeration of dozens, if not hundreds, of hands that made the decisions on what to include, what to highlight, and what to exclude—without any specific guidelines to make these important decisions.

As the executive who is in charge of the change effort, you want to minimize the number of steps between the actual data collection and yourself, at least for a portion of the sample. As that executive, you need to actively participate in part of the collection process, as this will allow you to see exactly what is being done to collect the information. Look at anything that might be confounding the results in between, and streamline it as much as possible, even if it slows the process. Remember, slow down to go fast. Executing too violently and too quickly will yield disastrous results when dealing with a change effort.

We are talking about changing workflow within an organization, but a product launch seems to be the easiest way to illustrate the point. The analogy of a product launch is that change within your internal organization is the product, and changing the way you do business is the result. You don't want to make excessive changes because you will burn everybody out. Start small and avoid the indirect routing problem. The customer in a change effort is an internal person or group. You are doing this with frontline employees, so it is not as difficult to get surveys done and reduce the routing as compared to when you are going out to the public at large.

How do you know where you are going if you don't know where you have been? One of the roadblocks is the interpretation of historical data and becoming seduced or biased by the individual understanding of history. Everybody thinks they know where they have been, but we have also all had the experience of daydreaming while driving and then realizing that we don't remember the last three miles.

Many times, that is how organizations work: we remember glimpses of landmarks or road signs along the path of our customer experience, but it is important that the change champion acknowledges that there are also some blank spots and tries to put together a composite of different people's interpretations of the history that is applicable to the proposed change effort. This is not unlike law enforcement recreating a crime scene by talking to as many witnesses as possible to get a composite view, with no one witness being more important than another. As an educated executive, you have the responsibility to weigh that input and decide what it means. Don't just say, "If I interview 65 people, I'm going to get 65 different stories." Well, yes, and your ability to thoughtfully weigh what you hear is why you are making the big bucks. That does not mean that you just take your experience and make the decision; you need to validate it. Then, you will know where you have been so that you can utilize the assets that are available to you to get where you believe you want to go.

So now we know where we have been. We can lament, and we can blame, or we can put those calories into moving forward. The cancer in most organizations is the drive to figure out who screwed up and to spend a great deal of time, money, and effort to assign blame. This is part of the human condition—additionally fraught with all kinds of political motivations that do not benefit the customer journey at all. Measurement tends to amplify the existence and the proliferation of politics for good reason: "I've got the goods on somebody, and I can assign blame." Resist that temptation, because it takes you nowhere and accomplishes nothing of value in the customer journey

Measurement should be used as carrots, not sticks. Measurement and forecasting is about trying to figure out where you're going because we know where we've been. The goal of measurement going forward is to set a new baseline and not to beat people over the head for where they have been. Once we know where we have been, how we got there really doesn't matter. What matters is where we are going and whether we are going to change how we get there.

This is the methodology for getting there. It is incremental change and small accretive behaviors that are based on measurement and attainment of a goal. Establish a baseline for where you want to be. Measure meticulously, and do something on a daily, weekly, quarterly, semi-annual, and annual basis to move forward toward that goal.

Do not make ambiguous goals. Your change efforts should include a goal that may or may not be attainable because it is so lofty, but it should have some stopgaps between where you are, which we have defined, and where you can be in order to get a small win. Like I said earlier, we would like to get a win in the first 90 days. Where is our 90-day win? Where is our 180-day win? Where is our 270-day win? Where is our 360-day win? And we are approaching our 720-day win; that is what we are really looking for. That is the big goal to which these earlier achievements have given momentum.

In my experience, when it comes to change, after a couple of quarters, instead of 90-day wins, you can start expecting 45-day wins. After a year of 45-day wins, you can start expecting 30-days wins—until you have a culture in which you can expect weekly wins. That is when you have really harnessed the winds of change, and your culture is adopting change as a matter of course and as a tactic—not as a necessary evil because the wheels have come off the cart here or there. It is important to get close to the baseline or the goal. Then you appraise it, and it is ever-improving.

The rest of it pretty well takes care of itself. You navigate toward a heading based off of the North Star. You are never going to get to the North Star, but you know you will get somewhere between here and there, and that is the whole point of goal setting. Your Big Hairy Audacious Goal (BHAG) should be so big that it is probably unattainable, but it is the journey of getting there that is all the fun.

TRIGGERS

Let's talk about the flipside of optimistic project planning—commonly known as the issues, risks, and mitigation log. When you are looking at a change effort, without dwelling on the cynical and the bad stuff, it is relevant and valuable to sit back and do some what-if scenario planning. Mistakes will be made, and you need to anticipate the high-probability failures and build mitigation plans for them. Forewarned is forearmed.

The idea is around building dissatisfaction signals into customer or target records. Target triggers are the anticipation of things that are going to shove a customer or a frontline employee back, either to the old way of doing things or to a new, potentially worse way. More often than not, what I have seen is that change effort does not get derailed because of flat-out denial; the change effort gets modified, which is more destructive because neither the naysayer nor the champion can really determine if the effort was or wasn't successful, since it wasn't really carried out fully—more of a "We did this, but not that" kind of effort. You must plan for this potentiality.

When you break your change effort down, you will find that certain components of it are more palatable than others. The less palatable ones must be considered. What if they do only four of the seven things? What is the likely result of that, and how are you going to deal with it? Better yet, how are you going to prevent it from happening?

The answer is: measure, measure, measure. All along this effort, you are going to measure against the baseline. You are going to be vigilant as to whether the baseline is holding, retreating, or advancing. Holding or advancing is good, but retreating needs to be examined. This is where you should take a page from agile methodologies of software development and where you want to do iterations of change as quickly as you possibly can. That will vary based on the size of the change effort and the size of the organization. The idea is to deploy with constant, gentle pressure. You have to back off when the change effort is retreating based on baseline and expectations and push a little harder when you are at status quo. You have perfect pressure while advancing at a constant rate.

This is not the time to speed things up. That is when companies make mistakes: "We've got a good thing going. Let's go faster. Faster, faster, faster." As you are harnessing the winds of change, you can't blow from the boat into the sail and make it go faster. You can't create the wind—it has to be organic.

Change begets change; the bigger the crowd, the more people show up for it. People begin to see the efficacy of your efforts and are more willing to invest and go along. And what do people do? People adopt what they help create. This is how you screw it up when you get some velocity and you go, "Good. We've got velocity. Let's push harder."

The human reaction is to push back against that pressure. Even those who were onboard will say, "Whoa, you're pushing too hard." But when they all join in, they are doing so because they are invested in the effort, see themselves as part of it and are excited to see it progress. The more they adopt, the more they help create. You don't need to push any harder. It will happen once you find the right space. Velocity takes care of itself.

As problems are resolved, be sure that you measure total customer journey and response time—including the time your customer spent waiting for parts to be delivered or on third party providers. The problem is, as humans, we try to create the illusion of simplicity by forcing out variables. It is not because we are stupid or simple. It is because we don't have the ability to process dozens, let alone hundreds, of variables in our heads. This is where technology is our friend, because the computer can process such figures. We can work smarter by searching for additional variables to feed into the measurement system, so they can be pivoted against one another to come up with a more robust measurement. This is what big data and analytics is about—leveraging the ability of technology, using computer processors to pivot multifaceted facts, and doing it faster all the time. You are going to need to stay vigilant on what is being resolved as well as the components of that resolution.

There is a tendency to say, "The analysis is done. I did this, and therefore, that happened. Now I feel like a valuable human being. May I have a raise?" But very little in life is the result of one individual's effort. In business, your successes result from the efforts of hundreds, if not thousands, of people. To claim credit personally is arrogant and counterproductive to the scaling and replication of the success, which is all that business cares about. Don't screw yourself by being arrogant; realize that there is more going on. Feed that data to the analytic engine. Just as you did when you came up with what to do, continue that vigilance and rigor around why something happened that was good (and get over yourself).

Don't forget regular maintenance. Attend to customer journey problems. It is easy to lose sight of those if you don't look at them daily. Customers, in this case, are synonymous with internal resources. The thought here is really an extension of the last one; when you find people doing good things or while good things are happening, it is critical that you make sure everybody involved in those good things gets rewarded and, more importantly, gets recognized for what they are doing right, because that demonstrates to all that you value their adoption efforts. That creates more wind in your sails in the form of more adoption, resulting in more velocity around change.

It is all about convincing your customers that you're the only company they want to buy from. A great customer journey doesn't have to be expensive. It is a matter of avoiding the detours along the way and rewarding those who are responsible for creating the experience and adopting change. At the end of the day, your frontline employees are the extension of your brand and the personification of your company.

CHAPTER 10

I ALREADY KNOW THAT!

Why consultants can help and how.

Any fool can know. The point is to understand.
—Albert Einstein

Consultants, independent counsel, internal and external committees, coaches, mentors, and mentor programs—these are all variations on the theme of calling in someone who can focus on the issue at hand, to the exclusion of all internal politics and conditions. A consultant cannot and will not solve all your problems, but they do bring objectivity and clarity to the issues.

Preconceptions and politics increase in both frequency and power as organizations get bigger. The number-one reason why consultants are used—and it is a good reason—is to attempt to remove politics from the information-gathering process that is required ahead of the implementation of change efforts. Another argument for hiring outside assistance is continuity of business because continuity is still king. You can't just stop doing business and say, "Okay. Give us six months while we change everything," unless you're horribly overstaffed, in which case you have other problems. Your people should be fully engaged in day-to-day operations. In order to implement a change effort, it makes sense to bring some people in from outside to augment your staff through the change and its adoption.

The deployment of just about every enterprise resource planning (ERP) system that has ever been attempted without outside help has flopped; it is only a question of how catastrophic it was. ERP are such long-term projects; even the outside team risks becoming internal.

You want your outside assistance to rotate if it is a long-term thing. That goes against human nature, too. Familiarity is great because it breeds trust. But it should be familiarity with your outside brand and not with individuals who represent the brand. You don't want your consultants to become part of the furniture, especially when they are supposed to be independent, outside consultants. You neither want to hire your friend nor do you want the consultant to become your friend.

Figure 15

It is also not a great idea to hire an "expert" in your field to helm this effort. If you want to change, then by the very nature of that decision, you don't want best practices from inside the industry. You want new practices that are uniquely your own, constructed for your organization, and that will increase your unique selling proposition and enhance your culture (see fig. 15).

What should you seek out in a consultant? You want commitment, creativity, candor, and integrity, as well as courage. Ask to see case studies; not ones that solve the problem that you have but those that show creativity in a difficult political environment. You want to see that they have done those things and demonstrated those qualities. Candor is the chief virtue; if they are missing candor, it doesn't matter if they have all of the other four. If they have candor, they don't need the other four, because what you are hiring them for is to essentially tell you how ugly the baby is and to have the commitment and creativity to stay with you while you fix it. But without candor, you have just hired your friend.

Frequently, outside consultants are hired to prove a point that the champion wants hammered home. They are not there to help decide what to do—they are there to assert the agenda. A lot of consultants are more than happy to do that. Many times, that is how vendors end up in that role. You get a trusted vendor, and they are brought in under the guise of being an expert. Lo and behold, they help you select their product! It is really amazing: "We looked high and low, and we came up with us."

Here are some things that you want to consider when you call a consultant. If you are in charge of a particular silo, then look inside that silo to say, "Who deals with the customer?" using the SIPOC definition of a customer. Keep in mind that your customer may be another internal department. What I generally ask people to bring to the conversation are some thoughts about how they currently engage with customers. If they are talking about the external customer, that is great, but that is usually limited to the customer service/call center piece.

If it is a virtual company or if it is a retail company, then it is about that one-to-one customer experience. Beyond that, we think about the internal customers from silo to silo and the touch points that particular silos may have with an external customer, exclusive of the point of sale or the point of service. What you are doing now and what seems to not be working? What are the complaints and the biggest cost centers?

The more important outcome is the transparency quotient that comes through during that discussion, which is the indicator of the relative change quotient. In other words, the more transparent you can be and the more open, honest, and thoughtful you are about your organization, the easier it is going to be to get to the next step, which is actually coming up with a change process that will move the needle.

If you don't want to change, then there isn't any reason to call anyone. If you are not willing to engage in what I believe is the most powerful and productive effort that you can engage in, then that is fine, because there are plenty of companies that are willing to tell you what you want to hear. But if you are interested in talking about what is good and what is bad, within the context of leveraging what is good and eradicating or changing what is bad for the better, then you are ready to dig in.

Size does not absolve you from the duty to care about your customer. Scaling care is a human thing, because at the end of the day, humans have to care about every customer. It is management's responsibility to give their people the tools and the tricks, the attitude, the culture, and the ecosystem to exist in an environment where they can care.

IN CLOSING

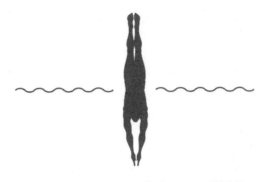

FREE CHANGE ... THE
HAWTHORNE EFFECT

Why it's okay to examine everything.

A manager is not a person who can do the work better
than his men; he is a person who can get his
men to do the work better than he can.
—Frederick W. Smith

No matter what you do, every action has an equal and
opposite reaction. Any time you start to examine something
or pay attention to something, you are going to generate some kind
of reaction. The Hawthorne Effect is also known as the Observer
Effect; the name comes from the Hawthorne Works, which was a
Western Electric Factory outside of Chicago. Henry Landsberger
coined the name in 1950, when he was analyzing experiments done

at Hawthorne in the late 1920s. At the time, management was testing the effects of lighting—sunlight or artificial light—on workers within the factory. Amazingly, during the course of the study, regardless of lighting type and level, the workers were more productive, but the heightened level of productivity slumped when the study was completed. Why?

What they found was that simply carrying out the study allowed their workers to feel more connected to the company because it showed them that the company cared about them. Businesses have dehumanized everything in their workflow to try to achieve greater efficiencies, and because they have made things more automated and rule heavy, the byproduct of these activities has been to beat the humanity out of the company. What the Hawthorne Effect tries to explain is the mere fact that management's examination will have an impact. Now, you are likely wondering whether that is a good or a bad thing, and my answer is that it depends on how you handle it, like anything when humans are involved.

If you approach change like a bull in a china shop, with the brute force deployment that we have talked so much about, then the caring that you have for the people in the ecosystem is lost because you have dehumanized the message. If you start talking about change in a way that is thoughtful and sensitive to the people, processes, and tools within the ecosystem that are going to have to change, that can, and in most cases will, have a positive effect in and of itself—remember the DNPS? If the change effort is perceived to be an attack or an attempt to toss blame or find fault, then you run the risk of turning the value of the Hawthorne Effect into a negative thing.

This is what happens with most change efforts, and it is why you need to call us, or somebody like us, to help you with the change effort. What we talk about is real, practical, and implementable material that quite frankly is a giant dose of common sense.

This book, our consultancy, and our measurement products are meant to be support for the internal effort of change and the betterment of businesses. They are not "set it and forget it," and any vendor that tells you they can do that is stealing your money. Change is hard, which is why it is so rare. That is why you hire outside people—to help you through those times when your commitment and your resolve get bludgeoned. It is the difference between having a standing appointment with a personal trainer, versus making a resolution to go to the gym more often. I suggest you find a trainer.

I want to thank you making it to the end of the book and make you an offer as a reward. So give us a call at Cliintel for half an hour of free consultation.

So what are you going to do? If you don't do anything else, call or email me and get your free consultation. Mention this book and this page number—oh, and please ask about jokes one and three from the preface!

Fearing change is essentially fearing success. When change presents itself to your company as essential and needed now...how will you react? Will you instigate and execute in the right way...or in a way that is self-defeating?

Do something; be first.

My contact information is below:

befirst@cliintel.com

720-200-3001